The Hurricane Pilot Who Became a Gestapo Agent

The Hurricane Pilot Who Became a Gestapo Agent

The Betrayal and Treachery of an RAF Sergeant

M S Morgan

First published in Great Britain in 2023 by
Air World
An imprint of
Pen & Sword Books Ltd
Yorkshire - Philadelphia

Copyright © M S Morgan, 2023

ISBN 978 1 39903 561 3

The rights of M S Morgan to be identified as the Author of this work has been asserted by him in accordance with the Copyright, Designs and Patents Act 1988.

A CIP catalogue record for this book is available from the British Library.

All rights reserved. No part of this book may be reproduced or transmitted in any form or by any means, electronic or mechanical, including photocopying, recording or by any information storage and retrieval system, without permission from the Publisher in writing.

Typeset in INDIA by IMPEC eSolutions
Printed and bound in the England by CPI Group (UK) Ltd, Croydon, CR0 4YY

Pen & Sword Books Limited incorporates the imprints of Archaeology, Atlas, Aviation, Battleground, Digital, Discovery, Family History, Fiction, History, Local, Local History, Maritime, Military, Military Classics, Politics, Select, Transport, True Crime, After the Battle, Air World, Claymore Press, Frontline Publishing, Leo Cooper, Remember When, Seaforth Publishing, The Praetorian Press, Wharncliffe Books, Wharncliffe Local History, Wharncliffe Transport, Wharncliffe True Crime and White Owl.

For a complete list of Pen & Sword titles please contact

PEN & SWORD BOOKS LIMITED
47 Church Street, Barnsley, South Yorkshire, S70 2AS, England
E-mail: enquiries@pen-and-sword.co.uk
Website: www.pen-and-sword.co.uk

or

PEN AND SWORD BOOKS
1950 Lawrence Rd, Havertown, PA 19083, USA
E-mail: uspen-and-sword@casematepublishers.com
Website: www.penandswordbooks.com

Contents

Introduction		vii
Chapter One	Flight of a traitor	1
Chapter Two	Augustin Preucil's evidence	21
Chapter Three	Max Brantal (Friend and close associate)	53
Chapter Four	Karel Čurda and Viliam Gerik (SOE traitors)	62
Chapter Five	Josef Chalupský (Gestapo interpreter)	70
Chapter Six	Other Gestapo-linked witnesses	77
Chapter Seven	The Terezín prisoners	89
Chapter Eight	Friends betrayed	100
Chapter Nine	Milena and Karel Tomanova	116
Chapter Ten	Others linked to Preucil	125
Chapter Eleven	Girlfriends and family	132
Chapter Twelve	Czech and RAFVR evidence	145
Chapter Thirteen	Incriminating documents from the court file	166
Chapter Fourteen	Post war reports, Muriel and the Preucil family	172
Chapter Fifteen	Who was Preucil's contact in the United Kingdom?	196

Chapter Sixteen	Could Preucil have been a double agent?	213
Appendix One	Sergeant Augustin Preucil's flights with 'A' Flight, 43 Squadron RAF	219
Appendix Two	Gestapo Officials linked to this story	221
Appendix Three	Czechoslovak/SOE (Arisaig) backed parachutist operations 1941–42	224
Appendix Four	Captured Czech aircrew held in Prague 1944: (Bold – confirmed or possibly in contact with Preucil)	230

Resources used in this book   233
Index   236

Introduction

The story contained within this book is 100 per cent true. The individuals involved and their accounts are genuine and have been identified after many months of research, delving through records in the archives of the United Kingdom and the Czech Republic.

The records in the Czech Republic amounted to many, many hundreds of pages of documents which I have translated and compared with the British records in the National Archives, the Royal Air Force and others. This is a story the vast majority of British people will not know today, over eighty years since the events occurred.

The story concerns one man in particular, Augustin Preucil also known to his family and friends as Gustav Preucil. He was a 26-year-old aviator from Czechoslovakia who, on first appearances, fled his homeland after Nazi Germany took control and created the Reich Protectorate of Bohemia and Moravia – part of Hitler's Greater Germany.

When Britain, under Prime Minister Neville Chamberlain, and France signed the 1938 Munich Agreement, they did so to avoid another world war. It allowed large numbers of ethnic Germans in the Sudetenland to come under the control of Berlin. However, by 1939 Germany had taken over the remainder of Czechoslovakia to form the new, larger, Reich Protectorate.

A great number of Czechs wanted freedom and after the army and air force were suspended in February 1939, hundreds of servicemen fled across the border to Poland, France and eventually to Britain, where they joined the armed forces. Augustin Preucil, as a pilot in the Czechoslovak air force, was one such man who moved to Poland, then France, and finally on to Britain, where he joined the RAF Volunteer Reserve.

After further training, he converted to Hawker Hurricanes and served with a fighter squadron, before undertaking a number of other roles including that of a flying instructor.

Augustin Preucil appeared to be just like the other young men who arrived in Britain to continue the war against Hitler. He appeared to be settled and even married an English girl in July 1941, but in September of that year, he was posted missing, believed killed, while training off the coast of Sunderland and Hartlepool.

Preucil's body was never recovered and nothing more was heard of him. His young wife received a war widows' pension and he became just another sad statistic of war.

However, Augustin Preucil was far from dead. He was in continental Europe serving the Gestapo, the infamous secret police and enforcers of the Nazi state. How he ended up serving the Gestapo and betraying his homeland, his adopted country and a new English wife, is a story that is strange yet true.

I first learned of Augustin Preucil while watching a television program in 2006. An avid student of military aviation, I also liked a good ghost story. So, when the *Most Haunted* television program advertised a ghost hunt at the North East Land, Sea and Air Museum (NELSAM) on the old RAF Usworth site near Sunderland, I had to watch it. (I also have family links to Sunderland and know the museum well.)

The resident psychic on the program stated that there was a man called Augustus or Augustine present in the museum hangar, who came from somewhere called Trebsin in Czechoslovakia. He wore RAF pilot's wings on his uniform, but the psychic kept seeing the Nazi swastika. He claimed the man was a spy and a thief who had been at RAF Usworth, stealing an aircraft and flying it back to Germany. Executed by hanging, he was in disgrace and haunts the old airfield, or what parts of it remained next to the new Nissan car factory.

Forgetting the issue of whether ghosts exist or not, I had never heard of this man nor the theft of an aircraft, let alone that he was a German spy. I therefore tried to research the story, but I could find very little about the man or the incident.

I soon found an old copy of the *Aeroplane* magazine from June 2003. This contained an article that told the story of Augustin Preucil and the fact that he had gone missing from RAF Usworth in September 1941. This was clearly the man I was looking for.

The article, written by historian and author Roy Nesbit, stated that together with Richard Chapman, they had discovered an old photographic image of a Hawker Hurricane in the Museum for Transport and Technology in Berlin. The image must have been taken before the night of 23/24 November 1943, as the museum and the greater part of its collection – including the Hurricane – was destroyed in an RAF bombing raid.

The aircraft in the photograph bore the squadron commander's pennant under the cockpit, had broken propellor blades and had the squadron markings PA-A on its fuselage, as well as the serial number W9147. Upon checking RAF records, the aircraft was found to have been on the establishment of 55 Operational Training Unit (OTU) at RAF Usworth near Sunderland. It had been missing, along with its pilot, Sergeant Augustin Preucil, since 18 September 1941.

The Hurricane appeared to have had a forced landing, although it was standing on its undercarriage in the image. The issue was how did a Hurricane missing on a training flight off the North East coast of England, end up in the wartime Berlin Transport and Technology Museum, and what happened to its Czech pilot?

Further enquiries by Roy Nesbit and Richard Chapman soon identified that Preucil had not only survived, but surrendered the aircraft to the Gestapo and was financially rewarded. After a visit to Berlin, he was returned to his homeland, where he worked for the Gestapo, assisting in the interrogation of downed Czechoslovakian airmen and betraying others.

Nesbit and Chapman had found an unbelievable story, but they could not access everything, could not identify the wife, or obtain a detailed RAF service history for Augustin Preucil.

After a number of years, I decided to try and piece the story together in early 2022, possibly with files and information that had not been available in 2003. Now nearly twenty years after the story first broke cover, I could access more information, including records about his wife in Sunderland, his RAF service record, his behaviour in the air force, his flight to the Continent and his betrayals. Having accessed the statements, records and court documents from the State Regional Archives in Prague, I set about the long task of translating them to build in detail, the story of Augustin Preucil and his life of treachery.

It was clear there was more to this story than previously reported. In the UK National Archives file on his disappearance, I found a letter from a renowned Polish RAF Battle of Britain pilot.

Antoni Glowacki had fought with 501 Squadron at Gravesend during the summer of 1940, before becoming an instructor with Augustin Preucil on 55 Operational Training Unit (OTU) at RAF Usworth. Glowacki survived the war before settling in New Zealand and it was from his adopted country in June 1977 that he wrote to the Air Ministry (Ministry of Defence) in London.

Glowacki explained that he had served in the RAF before joining 55 OTU as a fighter pilot instructor. In his broken English, he wrote:

> In summer of 1941 certain unusual incident took place which I intend to use in my future book of my flying stories. The 55 OTU trained young pilots of all nationalities and at that time we had 20 or so young Polish pilots under-going fighter training. Flight Lieutenant Royce was our CO. [Michael Elliott Royce was ex-504 Squadron and a Rolls-Royce test pilot, but in June 1941 he commanded 'B' Flight of 55 OTU at Usworth.]

Glowacki explained that there were two Czechoslovakian instructor pilots, one was Sergeant Prkal…

the other Czech Sergeant pilot (the name I forgotten) was involved in a weird incident during which he disappeared without a trace. At the day of the incident, he was a leader of a section of two Hurricanes, in a pair with a young sergeant pilot, on a gunnery training. Shortly after take-off one Hurricane was found crashed, south of Sunderland. The Hurricane was riddled with .303 bullets indicating that this aircraft was shot down. The other Hurricane with its Czech sergeant pilot, disappeared completely.

Later on, we have learned that the nearby radar station observed a single blip heading away from Sunderland area towards [the] South-East and the Belgian coast. The blip was lost at 200 miles.

After the war, we have learned that the Czech pilot landed in Belgium and gave himself up to Gestapo, who used him as a 'stool pigeon' in order to infiltrate the Belgian and French underground movements. The Czech contacted the above organisations and was helped by them to hide and escape towards Spain. On reaching the Spain he reported to the Gestapo all hiding places and the people who helped him in his escape. As a result, approximately 32 people were picked up and executed by the Gestapo. However, the Belgians and French realised that they were betrayed and decided to kill the traitor. A number of attempts on his life were made unsuccessfully. The Gestapo then send away their stool pigeon to Czechoslovakia where he entered the Czech resistance movement. He then betrayed the organisation and as a consequence approximately 50 Czech patriots were caught and executed by the Germans. At the end of the war, the Czech traitor was caught, tried and hanged publicly in Prague.

Glowacki said he could not remember the name of the Czech pilot, nor the Polish pilot who had been with him that day, but he had photographs of them both. He asked for their names and the date of the incident for his forthcoming book.

The British Ministry of Defence provided Glowacki with Preucil's name, but they could not identify the Polish pilot (probably because there is no record of him or his aircraft being shot down that day.) They also provided the date of the incident.

Sadly, Antoni Glowacki does not appear to have completed or published his memoirs, as he died in April 1980. Despite my best efforts via the Royal New Zealand Air Force Museum and the RNZAF Association, I have also been unable to make contact with any of his living relatives in New Zealand or locate his unfinished text and photographic images.

Antoni Glowacki's letter made some significant statements about Preucil's disappearance. Could they be true, or was there some fiction and rumour included in the account?

I found from research that twenty-two years earlier in 1955, Antoni Glowacki had been featured in a New Zealand newspaper as he trained the country's new jet fighter pilots. In the article, he recalled a slightly different account of Preucil's flight in 1941.

He recounted a Czech instructor landing his aircraft in the occupied Netherlands and giving himself up to the Germans. He then pretended to be a recently shot-down British airman so he could locate and identify members of the Dutch underground for the Nazis. Many of these men and women were captured and executed. His treachery was later discovered and he was 'shot by Dutch leaders'. Glowacki also told the media he was a keen amateur photographer and had an image of the Czech pilot at the British air station (almost certainly RAF Usworth).

Glowacki's account had changed somewhat between 1955 and 1977, but clearly there was still an under-lying story of treachery and betrayal.

As you will see, not only did Augustin Preucil betray his wife and the Royal Air Force, but he worked with some of the most renowned traitors in Czech history, including infamous Special Operations Executive (SOE) agents who betrayed others leading to many, many deaths.

Augustin Preucil is well-known as a traitor in his homeland and I hope he will be in this country after publishing this book.

I would like to thank the UK National Archives and the State Regional Archives in Prague for their assistance, as well as the RAF Museum at Hendon and the RNZAF Museum. In addition, my thanks go to the RAF service personnel records department and Dr Alastair Noble at the Air Historical Branch.

I would also like to thank Jaine Hilston (Historical TV Producer) for her assistance in pointing me in the right direction with some issues.

I must also praise Dr Henrik Chart at the museum in Arisaig, Scotland, for his invaluable advice regarding the Czech SOE agents who trained in the area.

Thanks also go to the staff at the North East Land, Sea and Air Museum (on the old RAF Usworth site) for their assistance.

My thanks also go to Josef 'Joe' Vochyán and the cestiarafaci website for allowing me to use the images of several Czechoslovak pilots; and last but not least to Tom Dolezal at the Free Czech Air Force Association for allowing me to use three images of Preucil and his colleagues in 1940 and 1941.

Most importantly, I would like to thank the son of Preucil's English wife Muriel, and his sister. He gave me considerable time and was very patient with my questions, I have not given their full names to protect their privacy.

This book will examine the evidence and the statements of Preucil and the large number of witnesses questioned by the Czech authorities after the war. It will also check the facts against other information held by various sources in the United Kingdom, while questioning whether there were links to other Nazi agents.

As a former Senior Investigating Officer in the police service, I have written this account in a manner similar to the way in which I wrote reports for prosecuting lawyers. It examines the evidence and the statements of the suspect and witnesses, before comparing the facts. It also looks at varying hypotheses. The first section will examine the overall story, before the following sections examine the evidence in detail from the suspect and witnesses.

The vast majority of the evidence contained within this book came from Czechoslovakian sources dated 1937–47. This information was translated and I would ask you to bear in mind, that although I believe the translation to be a good one, there may be some phrases and comments which did not translate into the literal Czech meaning. However, the main elements of this story are correct and any errors are purely accidental and no harm is meant is any way.

I hope you enjoy the story of Augustin Preucil. It is full of twists and turns, some of it straight out of the pages of a spy thriller, but remember, this story is true and the names were real people....

Chapter One

Flight of a traitor

Augustin Preucil, often known as Gusta or Gustav, was born in Trebsin to the southwest of Prague on 14 June 1914. (Remember the *Most Haunted* TV program psychic gave this town's name.) His father was also called Augustin Preucil and he was 55 years of age in 1941, while his mother was called Marie and aged 49. It is probably because father and son had the same first name, that he was known as Gustav.

The Preucils had moved to the address in Trebsin in September 1913 and Augustin junior was born the following summer. The family were practicing Roman Catholics and baby Augustin was baptised in the town church.

Records vary in relation to Preucil's father's occupation, and on his British marriage certificate in July 1941, it is shown as being a tailor, although some historians claim he had been a butcher. However, by 1944 when Augustin Preucil filled out some German paperwork, it appears he claimed his father was an inn-keeper.

Trebsin in 1939 was a small medieval town with a population of about 10,000. The family appear to have led a happy life, with the young Augustin attending the primary school in nearby Hradistek, before enrolling in the senior school in Neveklov. He was an average student and managed to learn some basic conversational French, this would be useful a few years later!

Preucil left school during the school year 1928/29 and went to work for a local grocery business as an assistant. The business owner was Vaclav Rehak and he appears to have been Augustin's uncle, as his mother's maiden name was also Rehak.

Augustin Preucil was interested in aviation and in 1935 he started flying lessons with the Civil Flight School at the Ministry of Public Works. This was situated on the old grass airfield at Letnany in the northeastern suburbs of Prague. Letnany was a centre of excellence for Czechoslovakian aviation in the 1930s and the Letov aircraft factory was situated next to the airfield. The Aerospace Research and Test Establishment (known as the VZLU) was also sited here, as was the CKD aircraft factory.

In 1935, Preucil qualified as a civilian pilot obtaining what was known as a 'sports licence'.

In October 1936, he was conscripted and joined the Military Aviation School in Prostejov the following month, before attending the non-commissioned officers' school in Cheb. After passing his course, his military flight training continued with the 3rd Aviation Regiment at Piestan and the 6th Aviation Regiment in Prague.

On 13 June 1937, (although his official record held in the 1947 court papers gives the date of 15 November 1937), he was posted to the 74th Air Regiment, Unit No. 6 – a reconnaissance squadron. He flew Avia biplanes and appears to have remained with them until 1938.

According to the record held within the court papers, on 16 April 1938 he was promoted to corporal.

As the Sudeten crises developed and worsened, the Czechoslovakian air force was partly mobilised on 21 May 1938.

On 1 October 1938, the file held in the court papers shows him missing three days of service and basically being absent without leave.

The mobilisation was increased to a full mobilisation on 23 September 1938, but on the 29th, Britain and France agreed to let Germany annex the Sudetenland with the Munich Agreement. Although Germany now controlled the Sudetenland, they still pursued other territorial claims over Czechoslovakia and as the political manoeuvring continued. Preucil was appointed a 'Field Pilot' on 24 February 1939.

Unfortunately, four days later Preucil and many of his colleagues were demobilised from the air force. Preucil had recently joined the 4th Aviation Fighter School to train as a fighter pilot.

As the German Army entered the wider Czech state, Augustin Preucil started to work for a clothing company called 'Rolny' in Vodickova Street in Prague.

The Luftwaffe was quick to confiscate all Czechoslovakian aircraft, airfields and facilities. It has long been reported that the head of the Luftwaffe – Hermann Göring – considered the pilots and engineers of the Czechoslovakian air force to be first rate, even if their aircraft were not of the same high standard as Luftwaffe machines. The Luftwaffe tried to recruit some of the Czech pilots into the Luftwaffe for non-combat roles such as ferrying and meteorological flights, but few men joined. A number who were recruited were instructed to fly aircraft to Germany, but when they took-off from Hradec Kralove airfield in Moravia, three flew straight to Poland, two to Russia and two others crashed, possibly deliberately.

4 The Hurricane Pilot Who Became a Gestapo Agent

It has been rumoured that Augustin Preucil applied to join the Luftwaffe, but his application was declined as he was not an ethnic German. This cannot be confirmed.

Augustin Preucil was clearly bored working for the clothing company and he heard that Brazil was employing pilots from Europe. He therefore went in June or early July 1939 to the Brazilian Consulate in Prague to offer his services and obtain a visa. Unfortunately for Preucil, he was detained by the Gestapo for attempting to leave the new Reich Protectorate illegally and taken to Petschek Palace (also known as Pecks Palace.) The building, formally a large Jewish bank, was now the headquarters of the Gestapo in Prague.

Preucil was interrogated by Inspektor Oskar Fleischer of the Gestapo and although exactly what was said and done is unknown, it concluded with Preucil being recruited to work as an agent for the Gestapo. (Most of the Gestapo files appear to have been destroyed before the conclusion of the war.)

Over the next couple of weeks, Augustin Preucil was given some rudimentary intelligence training by the Gestapo. He was to work as an undercover agent and sent to spy on his air force colleagues who had fled to Poland. He was to report back with their numbers, names and the locations of Czechoslovakian airmen to the Gestapo via an intermediary address.

On the night of 22/23 July 1939, the Gestapo took Preucil to the Polish border near Frystat. He was allowed to cross the border with gunshots fired into the air and shouts to make it appear an escape was under-way. Once over the border, Preucil would make his way to Krakow to join his Czech air force compatriots in a camp at Bronowice Male.

The Polish air force did not have time for so many new recruits, especially with Germany making threats towards Poland in early 1939. Therefore, the Czechoslovakian airmen travelled to France to offer them their 'services'. Preucil moved via Warsaw to the port of Gydina where he took a Swedish ship – the *Kastelholm* to Calais, arriving in late August 1939. The Czech airmen moved onto Paris with war just a few weeks away, but like many of his compatriots, Preucil was sent to join the French Foreign Legion, first of all in Agde and then at Sidi-bel-Addes in North Africa.

On 1 September 1939, Germany invaded Poland and three days later France and Britain declared war on Germany. Within days, the French realised that they had a good number of trained airmen in the Foreign Legion and recalled them to Chartres airfield near Paris. One of those men was Augustin Preucil.

Preucil arrived at Chartres at the start of October 1939 and was to train on French fighter aircraft with course No. 6. However, he was considered to be a poor pilot and indisciplined, especially on the ground, where he spent his time gambling and playing cards.

Preucil was still allegedly sending messages to the Gestapo as we shall see later. If he was still acting as a Gestapo agent, his behaviour did little to endear him to his senior officers and colleagues, while drawing attention to himself.

Preucil remained with the French training squadron at Chartres for seven months, but with the so-called 'Phoney War' over, the Germans were pushing into the Low Countries and northern France.

In June 1940 with northern France in German hands and the British Expeditionary Force evacuated from Dunkirk, Preucil moved southwards with other Czech pilots and many Frenchmen. Eventually, he was taken by ship to Gibraltar and then via a convoy to Liverpool, arriving on 7 July 1940.

Czechoslovakian air force personnel were initially taken to a camp at Beeston Castle in Cheshire and nearby Cholmondeley, but after a couple of days they were transferred to RAF Cosford. Sadly, the records for this period at RAF Cosford are no longer available, but we know that the station was used as a Czech depot.

I managed to access the RAF personnel file for Preucil. He is shown as enlisting in the RAF Volunteer Reserve on 24 July 1940 at RAF Cosford, serial number 787344 and immediately started his training as an aircraftsman second class (AC2). This basic training would have included some basic English lessons, RAF procedures, discipline, drill, rank structures and what the new recruits could expect from life in Britain.

It is also now known that the RAF, in conjunction with the British Security Services, carried out vetting of all new recruits from Czechoslovakia at Cosford and beyond. This was due to the fear that Nazi sympathisers and communists could infiltrate the service. Unfortunately, such vetting and security files are not available, but it appears Preucil passed his security checks because on 18 September 1940 (exactly a year before he fled), he was promoted to sergeant. Three days later he was posted to No. 6 Operational Training Unit (6 OTU) at RAF Sutton Bridge on the border of Lincolnshire and Norfolk. There he was to train and convert to Hawker Hurricane fighters.

Although no information is held in his personnel file or the OTU Operations Record Book, Preucil must have converted easily, as on the 7 October 1940 he was sent to 43 Squadron at RAF Usworth near Sunderland.

No. 43 Squadron had been heavily engaged during the Battle of Britain and was now resting, recuperating and training replacements in the North East of England.

There were a number of very experienced pilots on the squadron, including Flight Lieutenant Frank Carey who would become one of the most distinguished fighter pilots in the Royal Air Force.

Carey, who survived the war, wrote an autobiography in which he makes no mention of Preucil while at Usworth, or in relation to future events. This is surprising, as the squadron records show that he was his flight commander in the autumn of 1940 and must have heard of his later exploits.

The 43 Squadron Operations Record Book (ORB) for this period shows that Augustin Preucil was attached to 'A' Flight, and between 10 October and 12 November 1940 he flew thirty training sorties, totalling twenty-three hours and twenty minutes. He flew eight times with Flight Lieutenant Frank Carey, as well as with Czech pilots Sergeant Oldrich Fiafa, Rudolf Ptacek and Josef Pipa. Sadly, Fiafa and Ptacek did not survive the war, but Josef Pipa stayed with the squadron for two years. He survived the war and continued to serve in the RAF until 1962. Pipa died of heart failure at his home in Swindon in 1977.

Pipa did not write any personal memoirs and he does not appear to have ever mentioned the issue of Preucil with any historians, although he knew him and would have known of his later actions in 1941.

The 43 Squadron Operations Record Book does not give much detail about Preucil, except for flights, but there is a possible glimpse in the records of something untoward with Augustin Preucil.

On 13 October 1940, Preucil took-off with Pilot Officer Charles Edward Langdon and Sergeant Oldrich Fiafa at 15.00 hours. They were to undertake formation flying practice, but when the other two pilots returned, Preucil was not with them. He eventually arrived back at Usworth twenty minutes later. There is no explanation for his late arrival in the records. He had only just arrived at the station and could possibly have got lost, but he had two other pilots with him. Did he go off on a private indisciplined jaunt? Although he had only been at the station a week, could he have already met the girl from Sunderland he was later to marry and gone on a solo fly-past? We may never know why he was twenty minutes late, but it was unusual. (Langdon was killed off Malta in February 1941 with 261 Squadron.)

According to his RAF personnel file, Preucil remained with the squadron, but the record becomes confusing when it shows a further posting to 6 OTU back at RAF Sutton Bridge, but no actual joining date. Some historians have stated that he was posted to 605 Squadron, but there is no mention of his name contained within their squadron records. This lack of detail is surprising considering how well the RAF usually kept records.

The records also indicate another unit – 23 Maintenance Unit (23 MU) at RAF Aldergrove with a capital 'A' in a circle.

The unit flew and handled Airspeed Oxford aircraft – a change from Hurricanes. Again, there is no actual date of attachment. Was Preucil actually attached to No. 6 OTU and 23 MU?

Preucil's next dated posting according to his RAF file, was to 18 Maintenance Unit (18 MU) at RAF Dumfries on 10 March 1941, therefore it appears four months of service cannot be confirmed. This period, as well as the posting to RAF Dumfries, is worth remembering for later in the story.

RAF Dumfries and 18 Maintenance Unit also handled and flew Airspeed Oxford aircraft, as well as being the scrapping site for Vickers Wellington bombers. There was, therefore, an apparent continuation in flying Airspeed Oxfords – but why was a trained Hurricane pilot doing this when fighter pilots were in short supply? Had he been sent away due to his indiscipline?

On the 8 April 1941 Preucil moved again, this time to 10 Maintenance Unit (10 MU) at RAF Hullavington in Wiltshire. This was a storage unit for Airspeed Oxfords and Avro Ansons. Within a few days of arrival on 22 April, he appears to have been attached to an air ferry pool at nearby RAF Kemble.

After just a four-month period, where we cannot state exactly where and what Preucil was doing, we have three stations in just a matter of weeks. He eventually returned to No. 10 Maintenance Unit at Hullavington on 13 May 1941.

Some historians have claimed that on 11 June, Augustin Preucil was reprimanded after he performed a high-speed dive which damaged an unidentified aircraft's bomb bay doors. A door is reported to have broken off and struck the tail, damaging the starboard stabiliser. I have searched long and hard for a corroborating record, but I have been unable to find one. It is also surprising, as Oxford and Anson aircraft did not have bomb doors, so what could he have been flying?

Whatever did or did not happen on that day in June 1941, Preucil was on the move again five days later, 16 June. This time he was on his way back to RAF Usworth and Hawker Hurricanes, where he was to join 55 Operational Training Unit (55 OTU) as a flying instructor. Once again, this is a strange posting. This was a man who had not flown on operations with RAF Fighter Command and had apparently moved every few weeks or months. His RAF career up to that date had been anything but exemplary, but now he was to tutor young Hurricane pilots? If he had damaged an aircraft on 11 June, would he really be sent to a position of responsibility at Usworth just five days later? Personally I doubt it, and with no corroborating documents, I believe this alleged incidence of poor flying cannot be counted as a genuine event.

No. 55 Operational Training Unit like that at Sutton Bridge, trained Hurricane pilots before they joined frontline squadrons. The unit had a number of Polish and Czechoslovakian pilots and required people like Augustin Preucil and Antoni Glowacki to train them in tactics and air fighting.

Whether Augustin Preucil was still sending messages and intelligence back to the Gestapo at this time is unknown. If he was, it would certainly have been very difficult, having been posted to so many wide-spread and varied locations. If his 'handler' had been another air force man (or woman), they would have found it very difficult to follow him around the

United Kingdom. The same would have been true if they were a civilian agent handler.

According to his RAF record, Augustin Preucil was 5ft 9¾ inches tall. He had brown hair, green eyes with a fresh complexion and a 34 inch chest measurement. His spoken English was not perfect, but he managed to get by.

He had previously undergone surgery for a hernia and the removal of his appendix – both operations leaving the relevant scars. (Although no dates are given for this surgery, they could account for his regular transfers away from front line operations.)

On 2 July 1941, Augustin Preucil married a young English girl at Grange Church in Sunderland. The girl was 19-year-old Muriel Graham Kirby, who would later become a local schoolteacher. How long she had known Preucil is unclear, but it is probable she knew him from his previous posting to Usworth with 43 Squadron in late 1940. Preucil's address on the marriage certificate is shown as Hullavington (when he was with No. 10 MU) prior to his arrival at 55 OTU. This may have been his address when the marriage banns were first read, weeks before the actual event in July 1941.

Muriel lived with her family at Bainbridge Gardens, Sunderland. Her father, George Kirby, was a van driver and she had a number of brothers and sisters.

It is unclear whether they had a honeymoon as the 55 OTU Operations Record Book does not contain details of leave, neither does it show details of individual flights undertaken on a daily basis.

The two appear to have started married life together in Sunderland, but exactly where and how is unknown. Sadly, Muriel died in late 2006, but having spoken to her son, little is known about this part of her life and it was not discussed in later years.

On 27 July 1941 an event took place which may or may not have had a significant bearing on Augustin Preucil's later actions.

Preucil took-off in Hawker Hurricane serial number V7608 from Usworth. Unfortunately, the details are not included in the 55 OTU Operations Record Book so we cannot state exactly what type of flight he was performing. However, what we do know is that he failed to switch over his fuel tanks, causing the Hurricane's engine to falter and he made a forced landing at Houghton-le-Spring near Sunderland. Damage to the aircraft was minimal, or so it would seem, and a recovery team was sent out to collect the aircraft and return it to Usworth.

There has been reports that Preucil had a poor 'air discipline' record and this was the latest in a series of examples of poor airmanship. This, it has been claimed, was to have led to disciplinary action against Preucil, but no corroborating records have been found to exist. (I have searched the RAF court martial records held within the National Archives and there is no mention of Augustin Preucil. It is possible the charges were being prepared when he fled to the Continent, but are not listed within official records.)

Unfortunately, the same Hurricane that had been repaired was flown by Canadian Sergeant Frank P. Stamp on 15 August

1941, and dived from low cloud into the ground at Wardenshaw golf course at Houghton-le-Spring. Stamp was killed in the crash. An examination of the remains of the aircraft could find no defects and the blame appears to have been attributed to the pilot entering the cloud when he had been warned not to do so.

Whether Preucil was to be disciplined is unknown, but he carried on flying as an instructor. During late afternoon on 18 September 1941, he took off with an unidentified Polish sergeant pilot for dog-fighting practice. Preucil's aircraft was the commanding officer's personal machine marked with his CO's pennant below the cockpit. The Hurricane serial number W9147, was a Mark 1 version, built as part of a series from November 1940 to February 1941. It had served with 43 Squadron before being passed on to 55 OTU and it was therefore still quite a new aircraft in September 1941.

The Polish student pilot later reported that during the course of their practice dogfight he lost sight of Preucil's Hurricane, having seen flames coming from the Hurricane's radiator. This reportedly being over the sea off Sunderland and West Hartlepool.

The relevant RAF accident report card (AM Form 1180) gives these details, but also has the word 'wireless' written across it in capital letters. What this specifically refers to is unclear, but it is worth remembering when we discuss Preucil's interrogation by Czech investigators post-war.

The commanding officer of 55 OTU added a comment to the form, stating that he had written to Fighter Command HQ proposing that all Poles be sent to 58 OTU with other Allies, as it is difficult to get Poles to use the R/T correctly, especially when 'excited'.

The AM Form 1180 gives no indication of whether a search was made for Preucil, but we must expect one to have taken place that evening. The AM Form 1180 gives few details, but it does give a breakdown of hours flown by Augustin Preucil while in the RAF (it does not include those in Czechoslovakia and France.)

Initially, it showed a total of fifty hours on the Hurricane, but this was later changed to 109, seventy-three of which were in the previous six months (March–September 1941.)

The total number of hours on other types of aircraft was initially 100 hours, but this was changed to sixty-four, which included ten hours dual flying. Forty-nine of the 100 hours were in the previous six months.

The overall total, therefore, was 173 hours flying time in the United Kingdom. Together with his overseas time, he was quite an experienced pilot.

From these statistics, we can try to decipher what aircraft he was flying and when. It appears, if these assumptions are correct and basing it on the accident report card (AM Form 1180 for the Hurricane W9147), that after leaving 43 Squadron in November 1940, he under-took just eleven hours flying time in 117 days, about once every ten to eleven days.

In wartime Britain, this lack of flying time seems strange. Was he suspended for indisciplined flying? Was he ill, possibly through surgery, or was there another unrecorded reason for this? The hours are shown in the table below.

This is worth remembering as this story develops.

Period	Unit	Aircraft Type	Hours Flown
21 Sept – 7 Oct 1940	No. 6 OTU, RAF Sutton Bridge	Hurricane	12 hours and 40 minutes
7 Oct – 13 Nov 1940	43 Squadron, RAF Usworth	Hurricane	23 hours and 20 minutes
13 Nov – 10 Mar 1941	No. 6 OTU, RAF Sutton Bridge? No. 23 MU, RAF Aldergrove?	Hurricane Oxford	11 hours?
10 Mar – 8 Apr 1941	No. 18 MU, RAF Dumfries	Oxford	A total of 53 hours?
8 Apr – 22 Apr 1941	No. 10 MU, RAF Hullavington	Oxford	
22 Apr – 13 May 1941	Auxiliary Ferry Pool, RAF Kemble	Oxford/ Anson	
13 May – 16 Jun 1941	No. 10 MU, RAF Hullavington	Oxford	
16 Jun – 18 Sept 1941	No. 55 OTU, RAF Usworth	Hurricane	73 hours
Total flight time 109 hours on Hurricanes and sixty-four hours on Oxfords and Ansons.			

RAF Form 765C held in the UK National Archives (under reference AIR 81/9163) and completed the day after Preucil was reported missing, adds few further details to the story.

According to official records from September 1941, it appears the loss and the fate of Augustin Preucil were decided. He was reported as missing believed killed and his young wife of just two and a half months received the telegram all wives and families dreaded in wartime.

However, Preucil had not died in the North Sea. He had, in fact, flown on a southerly heading along the coast of the United Kingdom, before crossing the English Channel and North Sea. As his fuel began to run out, he made a forced landing in a field near the village of Ortho, close to La Roche in the Ardennes, Belgium. As his Hurricane came to a juddering halt, he sustained a small cut above his eye and was assisted by local villagers.

Nearly two weeks after his disappearance on 30 September, the War Office in London received a message through the intelligence services. This is believed to have been provided by the renowned Belgian resistance group code-named 'Clarence'.

The report stated that at 18.15 hours (GMT) on 18 September 1941 a single engine plane circled and then landed successfully at Ortho near La Roche. A pilot wearing an English uniform got out of the machine and was assisted by local civilians from a nearby farm. They gave him civilian clothing and hid him in the nearby woods. The pilot spoke French to the local farmers (he had learnt some French at school in Czechoslovakia).

The next day the local constable, aware of the incident, was said to have reported the matter to the Germans and they sent a large search party to look for the pilot. They searched the area, but failed to locate the pilot. Suddenly, the pilot broke cover and headed straight to the German troops and began to speak with them. He identified the farmers who had assisted him and they were immediately arrested. The resistance group also reported the serial number and coding of the aircraft – it was clear it was Preucil and his missing Hurricane.

Further reports were made by the Belgian resistance over the coming months. Those arrested were identified as Leon Charlier and his wife, as well as Armand Durand and another young male called Antoine. The four individuals were interrogated and tortured before Charlier and Durand were sentenced to death by the Gestapo. Their sentences were carried out on 21 January 1942 (Durand) and in September 1942 (Charlier.) The other two detainees were sentenced to a term of imprisonment. The first two people had died because of Augustin Preucil's treachery.

Leon Charlier and Armand Durand are commemorated on the war memorial outside the church of Saint Remy in Ortho, La Roche.

It appears that Preucil then returned to Czechoslovakia, and after confirming his identify with the Gestapo in Prague, he was taken to Berlin and the Luftwaffe headquarters on Prinz-Albrecht Strasse for a full debriefing. In time, he would be transferred back to Prague where he would become a Gestapo agent.

In London, the Czechoslovakian government in exile were soon alerted to the possible treachery of Preucil by 'British sources'. After consulting the Czech Air Force Inspectorate in London in early December 1941, the inspectorate replied stating that Preucil, 'Should have been brought before a court of law for air misconduct.'

The author of this secret message (Brigadier General K. Janousek) added that there was no news about his reliability, but he then added the following about Augustin Preucil's character: 'Personality: Talkative, boastful, likes to talk/explain about himself, likes to socialise with women, but he was married and his English is poor.'

The general concluded by stating that it was possible Preucil had got lost and accidently landed in Belgium. 'However, it is also possible to assume that he fled out of fear of the court.'

A few months later on 15 May 1942, the Czechoslovakian Air Force Inspectorate wrote to the Air Ministry. This was handled by an officer called E. Cowan at the S7 Casualty Unit B. He in turn contacted Squadron Leader Long at A.1.3(a)1 (intelligence section) stating that on 1 December 1941, the Czechs had received information that Preucil was alive, but there had been no further information since.

The intelligence services believed Preucil was alive, but no one knew where he was and what he was doing. His young wife Muriel, who had been receiving a war widows pension, had not been informed of these developments; she believed her husband to be dead – missing with no known grave.

It appears the trail went cold for the remainder of the war, although both the RAF and the Czechoslovakian authorities believed Preucil to be possibly alive and a traitor. They would have to wait until after the war's end to locate Augustin Preucil and work out what he had done.

In May 1945, the war came to an end and with Germany's surrender, the Czechoslovakian government and its military returned to their homeland. Their first actions were to locate and detain prominent Nazis like Karl Frank, the Secretary of

State for the Protectorate of Bohemia and Moravia, and senior elements of the Gestapo.

In addition, they had a list of names they knew from intelligence sources who needed to be found and arrested for collaboration with the Nazis and the Gestapo. Names on the list included Karel Čurda and Viliam Gerik, British trained SOE agents who had betrayed many of their colleagues, including the men who assassinated Reinhard Heydrich in 1942. The third name on the list was that of Augustin Preucil.

Over the next two years the Czechoslovakian authorities tracked down the victims and witnesses of Preucil's treachery. The witnesses included friends, air force colleagues, fellow prisoners and those unlucky enough to encounter the man.

What they discovered was astounding. Not only were his own actions unbelievable, but he also interacted with the likes of Karel Čurda and Viliam Gerik. How many people were betrayed by Preucil is unclear, but many died as a result of his treachery, while others suffered in concentration camps.

Some idea of the manner in which the search proceeded can be seen from a memorandum to Cetnica Police Station on 14 June 1945. It stated clearly, that Augustin Preucil was a collaborator whose father was supposed to be an inn-keeper in Mechenice. Preucil was described as being 30–35 years of age, about 180cm tall, slender build, with an oval face, aquiline nose with a prominent nasal bone (clearly his height was wrong.)

Preucil, it added, was supposed to be staying in the town of Davle, or in the vicinity, and was allegedly in possession of false documentation.

However, a further memorandum from Davle police station dated 22 June 1945, announced that Preucil had actually been detained on 19 May 1945 in Mechenice, probably by either Military Intelligence or the GPU from Prague. He had been taken to Prague and remained in custody awaiting a court appearance. The memo added that Preucil was born in Trebsin on 3 July 1914, the son of Augustin Preucil and Marie, maiden name Rehak. Their last address was apartment cp. 130 in Davle II.

Augustin Preucil was held at Pankrác Prison in Prague, a place where the Gestapo murdered many hundreds of their victims – many of them with the guillotine.

The following chapter will detail the words of Augustin Preucil, according to the interrogation and court documents held in the Czech Regional State Archives in Prague.

Chapter Two

Augustin Preucil's evidence

Augustin Preucil was arrested by Czech authorities on 19 May 1945. He was quickly interrogated to obtain a basic initial account from him, before the investigators could check and corroborate his story.

According to papers held in the Czech State Regional Archives in Prague, Preucil appears to have initially been interrogated on 20 May, possibly without legal representation. (The first note in the archive papers relating to any legal advice, is dated the 21 June 1945. That document, signed by Augustin Preucil, gives authority for a lawyer called František Koci to act on his behalf. On 19 November 1945, he signed another form for the advocate Dr Jaroslav Mellana.)

Preucil had plenty of time to consider his forthcoming interrogation while sat alone in his cell at Pankrác Prison. He did not know what information the authorities had about his work with the Gestapo or who they had spoken to. He also had no idea how many Gestapo officials, and those who knew of his treachery, had been detained and if they had talked. In addition, he did not know what incriminating Gestapo documents, if any, were in possession of his Czech captors.

Preucil knew he could expect a grilling about his disappearance from RAF Usworth in September 1941, but he had an account to explain that.

As mentioned, his first apparent formal interrogation took place on 20 May, just one day after his arrival at Pankrác Prison. Like any experienced investigators, the interrogators allowed their prisoner to talk and give his account without unpicking it or questioning his version of the facts. They could do that later and – if you pardon the pun – they would give him enough rope to hang himself.

The first interview was short in terms of the finer details, but it was enough to get his version of events on record before the detailed investigations began.

Preucil was quick to explain that after finishing school, he worked at an inn and learned butchery from his uncle (Vaclav Rehak) for two years – this would have been at his shop.

In 1935, Preucil said he signed-up for pilot training at the private flying school in Letnany near Prague. He then joined the Czechoslovakian air force in 1936 at Prostejov, before being sent to what he called a 'conscript school' for two months. After that he returned to Prostejov, where he completed his elementary military flying training.

He continued to explain that after his elementary training, he went to the 3rd Regiment at Piestan, before joining the 6th Aviation Regiment in Prague. Finally, he was sent to join the 74th Field Squadron in Hradec in the autumn of 1938 and on to the 4th Aviation School in Prague to train as a fighter pilot. Unfortunately, according to Preucil, as soon as his training was completed, he moved to the 1st Aviation Regiment in Milovice in February 1939, but was demobilised due to the German occupation. He therefore returned to civilian life and found a new vocation.

Augustin Preucil told the interviewing officers that in July 1939, he was arrested by the Gestapo at the Brazilian Consulate. He had been in a restaurant in Vaellava Square, Senflok when a lady approached him and asked him why he was not in Poland yet; Pepik Fuller and Honza Svoboda were already there and a man called Karel had sent them there. Preucil told the interrogators that he told this woman he was going to Brazil. He left the restaurant and went to the Brazilian Consulate where he made enquiries about moving to Brazil and handed over his documents. When he left the Consulate office, he was detained by the Gestapo who arrested him for illegally attempting to leave the Protectorate of Bohemia and Moravia. Straight away they demanded he tell them who 'Karel' was, and he recognised one of the Gestapo as a customer from the restaurant in Vaellava Square, where he had spoken with the woman.

Preucil was taken to the Gestapo headquarters at the Petschek Palace in Prague. He told the investigators he was repeatedly questioned and returned with Gestapo officers to the restaurant, where they demanded he identify Karel if he saw him. He agreed that he would raise his hand or a handkerchief to shoulder level if Karel arrived. Karel, whose full name Preucil said he did not know, worked with another man called Miksovsky, sending people across the border to Poland. Miksovsky owned the restaurant, but Preucil claimed he never identified this man to the Gestapo. Eventually, with no one being identified, Preucil was returned to the Petschek Palace and a cell in the basement.

Initially, in this first interview with the Czech investigators, Preucil did not say he was tortured or threatened, but he was informed he was to work for the Gestapo.

On 22 July 1939, he was taken by car to the Polish border and told he was to go on a mission for the Gestapo. If he didn't go, he would be sent to a concentration camp.

Preucil said he was given the address of a dentist and told to send details by post of how many Czech airmen there were in Poland. The name of the man he was to write to was Smetana Bedřich; however, this may have been a cover name – Smetana Bedřich being a renowned nineteenth-century Czech composer.

He was directed to write the letter like any normal letter, but in it he would state how many litres of milk he had sold. This was the code for the number of Czech airmen present in Poland.

The Gestapo men gave Preucil 50 Czech Koruna for his overnight lodgings and sent him across the border near Hranice and Frystat. When he crossed the border, he was quickly detained by the Polish police and sent to an internment camp at Bronowice Male.

Preucil told the investigators that he stayed in the camp for about two weeks and admitted sending two messages back to Smetana Bedřich, however he claimed they were just greetings and did not contain any information about Czech personnel.

Preucil and a number of other Czech airmen were then moved to Gdynia and sent by ship to Calais in France. He was taken to Paris, but then he had to join the French Foreign Legion. In this initial interview he stated that he later enlisted in the French Air Force and after training, joined a French fighter squadron. When France fell, he went by ship to England in July 1940, joining a British fighter squadron for training, but he could not remember the commanding officer's name.

Preucil did not give any further details of his time in England during this first interview, instead he moved straight onto his flight to Belgium on 18 September 1941.

He told the interviewers that he was sent on a flight with a Polish pilot, who was supposed to practice attacks. The conditions were bad with a thick fog and they flew far out to sea, losing radio contact with their base at Usworth near Sunderland. The two pilots got lost and Preucil says he flew on a southerly course, expecting at some point to see the English coastline, which he knew ran in a rough south-easterly direction. Eventually, he spotted land and assumed he was above England; he soon ran out of fuel and made a forced-landing. He then discovered he was in Belgium, near the town of Artolin.

As he landed, Preucil said he cut his head over the right eye. Two citizens of a nearby village, the name of which he could not remember, took him to their home and gave him civilian clothes. They hid him overnight, but the Germans started to look for him in the early hours, so he fled into a nearby forest. Despite hiding, he claimed he was located by the German soldiers and arrested.

Preucil told the interviewers that he was treated at the local hospital as well as being interrogated in Brussels. He told them the Germans asked him about his commanders, new types of aircraft, the road networks in England and whether they are defended against tanks. He explained that he had 'tried hard not to tell them the truth'. (This comment makes one wonder, if he suspected they may have had an old Gestapo or Luftwaffe report in their possession, detailing the information he had supplied.)

On or about the 28 September 1941, Preucil says he was taken to Berlin where he was interrogated again, before being taken by train back to Prague.

In Prague he was taken to the Gestapo headquarters where he had previously been detained. Again, he was interrogated and asked about specific Czechoslovakian airmen in Poland and France. He claimed he had denied knowing any of these men.

On 30 September 1941, Preucil was released and went to live and work at his parents' home in Trebsin. He claimed he was released because the Gestapo thought he could not work for them. (This was a strange comment, as by late 1941, a number of Czech airmen had been captured and sent to PoW camps.)

In late 1941, Preucil claimed two members of the Gestapo arrived at his parents' home and took him back to their headquarters in Prague. There he was given a reward of 10,000 Reichsmarks and asked to sign a receipt. Preucil claimed the Gestapo didn't say what the money was for, or its purpose! He then went home to Trebsin taking the money with him.

Preucil went on to say that in the month of April 1942, Czech agents launched by the English parachuted into the country. One of these men, by the name of Gerik, volunteered to work for the Prague Gestapo. Two members of the Gestapo collected Preucil and took him to their Prague headquarters where he was confronted with Gerik to see if they knew one another. The two men did not recognise one another and the meeting was concluded and Preucil was allowed to leave the building.

In June 1942, another parachutist called Karel Čurda signed up to the Gestapo and once again, Preucil claimed he was called in to confront this man. Again, Preucil said they did not recognise one-another and he left the building.

Preucil added that in the autumn of 1942, the man called Gerik brought a letter to a girl called Milena Tomanova. The letter came from a man called Modrak who was serving in England. Milena was warned by Preucil's good friend Max Brantal that this man Gerik could not be trusted as he worked for the Gestapo. Preucil upon meeting with the girl, also told her that Gerik could not be trusted and that she should report him to the Gestapo. Preucil said he was fearful that the girl would tell the Gestapo about his tip-off, so to buy her silence, he bought her a number of gifts totalling 38,000 Czech Koruna.

As the interrogation continued, Preucil left this matter and moved on a year to 2 November 1943. He said he was arrested by the Gestapo on suspicion of being a British agent and taken to the Terezín concentration camp. He was held there for six months before being released and taken back to Prague. Once in the city, he was taken to a control office to work, looking after General Engler and other high-ranking Czechoslovakian officials. He was expected to observe these men and make reports to the Gestapo about their activities. At this time, Preucil did not give details of what he did in this role, but he said he had stopped working there on 15 January 1945.

Preucil continued to chat with his interrogators and added that the Gestapo did not pay him, but that he was paid a monthly salary of 1,800 Crowns (Koruna) for the routine office work he under-took.

Preucil stated that Gerik, who had worked for the Gestapo, and Karel Čurda, with an alias of Josef Jerhot, betrayed the parachutists who assassinated Reinhard Heydrich in 1942. They received 5,000,000 Crowns (Koruna) for this treachery.

Smetana Bedřich, the dentist to whom he was to report, had an address at Husova Street, Ziskov. There were other people he said were traitors and gave the name of Olda Saifer from Avia. He had been looking for Preucil's close friend and ex-air force colleague, Max Brantal. Another was a man called Strzinek, he was the son of a forester from Cisoviec, he had the photographic images of Russian paratroopers and knew there was a 300,000 Crowns (Koruna) reward for their capture. Milan Hajke also worked for the Gestapo and a woman called Ella Fortikova had a brother in the German army (in time it would transpire she was actually an ex-girlfriend of Preucil.)

Preucil moved on to explain what had occurred in England. He said he had informed a Mr Berounsky and Dr Klouda, whose father was a Czech senator, that the Germans had wanted him to work for them, but he did not say what their response was, or when and where he told them of this.

Preucil said he was sent to a front-line English squadron, before working on training pilots. He then went to the parachutist training centre at Dumfries as a tutor (there was no parachute training centre at Dumfries). He also said he worked in the Maintenance Unit at Dumfries (which was located there).

He claimed the training school taught two groups: one for espionage and the other, terrorist and diversion tactics. They also taught the use of explosives and mines, as well as how to attack people and use the Browning pistol. He even explained that they were taught to hide the pistol in their inside document pocket, so that if stopped, they could access the pistol as if they were taking out their identification card.

Preucil told the interviewers that he was then recalled to Sunderland (RAF Usworth) and joined the 'secret police'. This was arranged via his wife's brother-in-law, who was a member of the British secret service, although he gave no name for his brother-in-law.

Preucil claimed to have been trained to withstand interrogation by the British, so he would know what to do if he fell into the hands of the Gestapo. The trainers wore Gestapo uniforms and civilian clothing during the interrogation training. He claimed he was told that when eventually sent back to the Germans, he should make contact with them – but he ended up with them sooner than he had expected with the Hurricane!

Preucil's role was to identify the Prague Gestapo officers and possible traitor parachutists who were joining the Germans. He was not to tell anyone anything, not even the Czechs, and would only report to the British via his brother-in-law. Preucil claimed to have tracked down Gerik and Čurda, as well as the other traitor parachutists Kindl and Grabovsky. He also named František Pospisil.

He went on to name a number of Gestapo officers, giving the names Fuchs (Adolf Fuchs), Schulz (Wilhem Schultze), Kommissar Wilhelm Leimer, Bunger, Inspector Oskar Fleischer, Diabo (Heinz Diabo), interpreter Josef Chalupský, Jiri Pitter, David (Bohuslav David), Inspector Muller (Julius Reidel Muller), Jan Metzner and Bauer (Bedřich Bauer.) He claimed Kommissar Leimer had released three captured parachutists so they could become informers for the Gestapo.

A Gestapo man called Omann had told him this in November 1944, but he could not remember the names of the three men.

Finally, Preucil claimed that he was working for the English intelligence services and the Czechs knew nothing about it. He then added that the English intelligence services were directed against the USSR, and their opinions were clear. This final sentence is one that should be remembered for later in this book. The Soviet army was in control of most of Czechoslovakia and Prague, the Uprising having only ended a few days before this interview with the Czech officers.

Augustin Preucil's first interview came to a close. In summary, he claimed he had been trained by the British secret service via his wife's brother-in-law. He had not been ready for deployment to Europe at the time and had carried on with his RAF service. His ultimate task when deployed would have been to identify the Gestapo in Prague and any parachutists working for them.

Unfortunately, he had got lost in the fog and accidentally landed his Hurricane in Belgium. He was captured, and when interrogated had not given away any information due to his training. He was taken back to Prague and confronted with the traitors Viliam Gerik and Karel Čurda, but that was all. He was then allowed to leave and go home. Later, he was rearrested as a suspected British agent and imprisoned in the Terezín concentration camp for six months.

The interviewing officers already knew about the landing in Belgium and the allegation he had betrayed the local Belgian civilians. It was hard for the Czech investigators to believe the reward was not for some treachery by Preucil and that he had not been working for the Gestapo; and why release him from Terezín if they really believed he was a British agent? Preucil certainly knew the names of a good number of Gestapo officers and officials.

Finally, was he really a British agent? Would the British not inform their Czech allies about this? There was a large amount of investigation required to get to the bottom of this man's apparent treachery.

Augustin Preucil's interrogation continued over the coming weeks and months, and he started to tell the investigators more about the Gestapo. He claimed that the Gestapo knew what was 'being done in England', because they had their own people there. Preucil said he could prove this because he had seen a photograph of the pilot nephew of General Kutovas in the Gestapo building. This photograph had been sent to the Prague Gestapo by one of their agents in England.

On another occasion the Gestapo had asked Preucil about 'Captain' Duda (believed to be Flight Lieutenant Josef Duda of 312 (Czech) Squadron, No. 4 Ferry Pilots Pool and No. 8 Maintenance Unit at Little Rissington), and whether he was alive and well in England. Preucil claimed that some of Duda's reports were visible on the table before him and the Gestapo men were happy and smiled when he said Duda was healthy and still working. The Czech interpreter present throughout the meeting told Preucil that Duda was working for the Gestapo. Preucil also claimed the Gestapo had files on Major Karel Šifner of the Czechoslovakian air force, who was in England.

On 22 May 1945, Preucil was given another short interview to confirm and clarify some of the earlier comments.

On 12 June 1945, Preucil was interviewed again. This time he gave details of his time in France.

He had been at Chartres airfield near Paris, where he claimed he had informed a number of people about his enforced work with the Gestapo and provided the name and address of his contact, Smetana Bedřich. The individuals he claimed to have told included Captain Provaznik, the former Czechoslovak air attaché to Yugoslavia.

In France his commanding officer had been Franc Plukovnik Nouville, and his senior Czech air force officers were Major Jan Ambrus and Flight Major Alexander Hess (both men would fly with the RAF and were at Chartres near Paris in May and June 1940).

Preucil claimed that he was sent on a Swedish ship to England in July 1940. A squadron was formed of Czechoslovakian pilots, 310 (Czech) Squadron under Flight Major Alexander Hess, but there was no room for all the Czech pilots and Preucil went to a British squadron (43 Squadron). Preucil went on to claim to have taken part in action – but there are no combat claims or losses recorded for the unit throughout the period he was with 43 Squadron.

While based in Sunderland, Preucil says he met and married a local girl called Muriel Graham Kirby on 2 July 1941.

He repeated his account of the landing in Belgium, saying he got lost in the cloud and ran out of fuel. He had lost sight of the accompanying Polish pilot. This time, Preucil added that his Hurricane turned upside down when he landed, injuring himself above the right eye. The under-carriage was damaged and the propellers broke off. The left wing was also allegedly damaged in the forced landing (remember, at this time no one knew the Hurricane had been taken virtually intact to the Berlin Museum, where it was destroyed in a 1943 air raid).

Preucil stated that a number of Belgian villagers approached him and, in English, he asked them where he was. Clearly, they did not understand him, so he used some of his schoolboy French and discovered he was in occupied Belgium. He told them he was an RAF pilot and they took him to their village, where they hid his uniform and gave him civilian clothes. His wound was also washed and treated by a villager.

The villagers, according to Preucil, told him to hide until a plane arrived which would take him back to England (via a Lysander perhaps). One of the villagers noted his aircraft codes and its serial number before telling him they would inform England. Preucil told the investigators that he had told them to remove the aircraft's radio and the machine guns before setting fire to the machine.

The next morning, the villagers took him out of the house as the Germans were searching for the downed pilot. Preucil said he was hidden in the forest, but soon arrested – due to a Belgian telling the Germans where he was hiding, he believed.

Preucil said he was taken straight to Brussels and questioned about military measures in England, the roads and road-blocks in the southeast. The Germans did not ask him much about the RAF, as they appeared in his opinion to be very well informed, he quickly added.

The Gestapo interrogators in Brussels knew he was a Czech and used a Slovak pharmacist as an interpreter. Initially Preucil says he denied being a Czechoslovakian pilot, but they had his uniform and parachute, the tunic having a 'Czechoslovakia' badge on each shoulder. Fearing he would be shot as a spy, Preucil said he finally admitted to being a Czech pilot, before divulging that he actually worked for the Gestapo in Prague.

Preucil claimed to have told his German interrogators, that he had an English wife who was wealthy with her own apartment in Sunderland. He was taken to Berlin and handed over to the local Gestapo, who took him back to Prague.

In Prague he was then given 10,000 Koruna for flying the Hurricane to Belgium. Before the Gestapo eventually released him, they showed him a series of photographic images of Czechoslovakian airmen and soldiers believed to be in Britain. Preucil claimed he did not know them, but he did recognise two men he knew as pilots Brejcha and Hanzlicek. He stated he did not identify them to the Gestapo and kept their identities secret. (The men are believed to have been Sergeant Vaclav Brejcha, who flew at Chartres and went to England. He flew with Preucil in 43 Squadron at Usworth in late 1940, but he was killed in a flying accident off the Norfolk coast in June 1941. The other pilot was Otto Hanzlicek, who was also at Chartres and flew with 312 (Czech) Squadron. He was killed on 10 October 1940, when his Hurricane caught fire and crashed. Hanzlicek baled out, but drowned in the River Mersey near Speke airport, Liverpool.)

Preucil was happy to talk with the Czech investigators and informed them that he was shown old yearbook images from the training school at Prostejov, but thankfully the Gestapo did not have the yearbook for his year.

Preucil claimed he was asked by the Gestapo if he knew a Major Karel Šifner. He asked the Gestapo's interpreter what was so interesting about this Šifner, but was told it would be of no interest to him and could cost him his life! (Karel Šifner actually worked for the Czech Ministry of National Defence – MNO in London and personally knew Preucil – see a later chapter.)

Preucil then repeated an earlier comment, and the fact the Gestapo had asked him about Captain Duda. This time he claimed to have told the Gestapo he had never seen Duda, this contradicts his initial statement, when he said he told the Gestapo that Duda was alive and well in England. He then added once again that a Gestapo official stated Duda was working for them.

The Gestapo men spoke only German and Preucil said he could understand just a few parts of their conversation.

The Gestapo also asked Preucil about a Lieutenant Kembal. They appeared to infer he was a Czech air force pilot-observer, but he was now working for the Gestapo. Preucil told the Czech investigators that he had known a Sergeant Kembal in Poland, where he had been suspected of spying. He was the son of a farmer and a teacher from Moravia-Ostrava, but when he asked the Gestapo officers about Kembal, they were taken aback and quickly changed the subject. (I have been unable to identify this person.)

Preucil told his Czech interviewers that he had spoken to the Gestapo about the French Foreign Legion, but they laughed at the fact Czechs had to join the Legion. They then stated that they would take care of Osusky and Laval. They also added that they had known that the Czech President in exile, Eduard Benes, would not go to France in the winter of 1939. (Stefan

Osusky was the Czechoslovakian ambassador to France. He signed the agreement on behalf of his nation, allowing pilots like Preucil to enter the French Air Force in October 1939. He later escaped to London in July 1940, where he worked at the MNO offices and probably knew Major Šifner and heard of Preucil.)

Preucil repeated that he had gone home upon release to his parents in Trebsin, on 30 September 1941. This time, he added that he had told his parents what had happened to him. His father had warned him not to do anything for the Germans, and to think of his parents' personal safety.

Preucil also elaborated on his initial account of two Gestapo men coming to Trebsin to collect him in late 1941. This time, he claimed they arrived on 24 December 1941. They took him back to Prague where they paid him 10,000 Reichsmarks, which he accepted and for which he signed a receipt. Preucil claimed he did not know what the money was for, but he assumed it was for the English aircraft he had force-landed in Belgium.

The Gestapo wanted him to speak to Czech airmen in England on the public radio, but Preucil told the Czech investigators he had to refuse to do this on the grounds of his young wife's safety in England, which the Gestapo apparently accepted.

Preucil continued to chat with the Czech interrogators and turned to the subject of Viliam Gerik. (Gerik was a Special Operations Executive (SOE) agent, dropped in late March 1942 as part of the three-man team code-named Operation Zinc. He almost immediately became separated from his colleagues and surrendered himself to the police. As a Slovak, he expected to be well treated when he surrendered on 4 April 1942, but he was handed straight over to the Gestapo.)

Preucil again stated that in April 1942, he was called to the Gestapo headquarters two or three times. On one of these occasions, he saw a young man sitting on a bench. He was told by an official that this man was a parachutist from England and his name was Gerik. Preucil was not to talk about him. Preucil claimed he did not speak with Gerik in the Gestapo headquarters and he believed the Gestapo just wanted to see if the man recognised him.

Preucil also claimed that on an earlier visit, the Gestapo had shown him the photographic images of twelve Czechoslovakian paratroopers (SOE agents) in England. They asked if he knew any of them, but he did not. A Gestapo official then stated that the twelve men would be dropped into the Protectorate in about fourteen days – an admission Preucil says surprised him. (Was this information given by Viliam Gerik to the Gestapo?)

The Gestapo eventually confronted Preucil with Viliam Gerik in Petschek Palace. Preucil claimed that he asked Gerik in English if he was a parachutist, but Gerik said he was not and had already registered with the police. In response, Gerik challenged Preucil saying that it was possible 'he' was a parachutist or an agent. Preucil did not expand upon this issue.

After Reinhard Heydrich was assassinated (the attack was on 27 May and he died on 4 June 1942), Preucil claimed he was called in once again by the Gestapo. He was confronted with another man – this one was called Čurda. (Karel Čurda was a member of the SOE group code-named 'Out-distance' and dropped into the Protectorate on the same night as Viliam Gerik in March. The two men undoubtedly knew one another from their time in Britain. Karel had surrendered to the Gestapo when he walked into their Prague headquarters on 16 June. He gave information that led to the discovery of the 'Jindra' resistance group which supported the SOE parachutists. This ultimately led to their deaths of the SOE agents in the church of St Cyril and St Methodius in Prague on 18 June 1942.) Having already spoken about Karel Čurda in his earlier interviews, this time Preucil went into the matter in more depth.

Preucil had been confronted with Čurda, but didn't know him. He was allowed to leave by the Gestapo, but within the next two weeks, he was in Franuzka Street when he was tapped on the shoulder from behind. When he turned around, he saw a man he did not initially recognise. The man asked why Preucil did not recognise him, before stating he was Karel Čurda and that they had met in the Gestapo building.

Čurda stated he was a parachutist from England and had known the Heydrich assassins personally before their deaths in the church. Preucil also claimed that Čurda admitted that he had given information about the Moravian family (the Jindra group) who the parachutists had stayed with.

Preucil claimed that Karel Čurda had told him he had been rewarded for his information and providing the parachutists' passwords and radio codes. He received 5,000,000 Koruna for this, while Viliam Gerik had been similarly rewarded by the Gestapo for his assistance.

It is clear that a friendship developed between the two, as Preucil added that Karel Čurda had taken him back to his apartment where they continued to talk.

In the apartment, Preucil discovered that Čurda now had an alias of Karel Jerhot – given to him by the Gestapo. The two men became regular contacts and Preucil says he visited Čurda's apartment a number of times.

Čurda had fully admitted helping with the arrest of fellow SOE parachutist František Pospisil, leading him to the Gestapo. He had told Pospisil that a lieutenant was going to meet him in the Koruna Arcade in Prague, but the Gestapo was waiting for him. (František Pospisil was another SOE agent dropped as part of the Bivouac group on the night of 27/28 April 1942. František was the cousin of Lieutenant Adolf Opalka – one of those killed in the church in Prague. Within days of the drop, his two fellow agents were captured, but he escaped and remained at large until lured to Prague by Karel Čurda and fellow Czech traitor, Jaroslav Nachtmann. He was finally detained on 10 February 1943. Pospisil refused to cooperate and assist the Gestapo, ending up in the Terezín concentration camp where he was executed without trial on 28 October 1944. He would have been in the camp while Preucil was in the same establishment.)

Preucil told the Czech interviewers that he wanted to overpower Čurda and shoot him for this treachery. Once they were drinking in Čurda's apartment and Preucil pretended to be drunk. He invited Čurda to shoot the empty bottle with one of his Gestapo issued pistols. Preucil claimed they both fired a shot at the bottle, but the shots caused 'a lot of attention' from surrounding residents and he knew he could not shoot Karel Čurda in the apartment and hope to escape the neighbours' attention.

Preucil again stated he had contacted his long-term friends Max Brantal and Ivan Malik in Prague. He told them about Čurda and Gerik betraying the Heydrich assassins and their Gestapo rewards. He also told them that if he did not survive the war, they must ensure that both Čurda and Gerik were brought to justice.

Preucil then moved on to elaborate further on the story of Viliam Gerik and Milena Tomanova.

He said he learned from Max Brantal of an associate named Milena Tomanova. In the winter of 1942, Brantal visited Preucil. He was, according to Preucil, very upset and asked for his advice.

Milena Tomanova had received a letter from her sister, Irena's fiancé (a man called Modrak.) He was in the Czechoslovakian army in England. The family feared a Gestapo trap and when the means of delivery was stated – a man called Gerik – Brantal immediately contacted Preucil for help. (This was because Preucil had already confided in Max Brantal about this man being a traitor.)

Preucil said he went with Max Brantal to meet with Irena in Prague, telling her Gerik was a traitor and apparently working against her on the orders of the Gestapo. Preucil advised her to report Gerik to the police to protect herself and her family, and similarly advised the girl's father when he met with him.

Preucil told his Czech interrogators that by this time he was concerned that the Gestapo were watching him. He had been called in several times, but he did not know what they wanted from him.

Eventually according to Preucil, he decided with Max Brantal and Ivan Malik, to kill Čurda and Gerik. It was decided they would shoot them both, as Preucil had a gun given to him by the Gestapo. They needed to be shot together, but they could not locate Gerik. (The fact Preucil now admitted the Gestapo had given him a gun, must have been a shock revelation to the Czech investigators.)

Preucil said he had introduced Max Brantal to Karel Čurda in a restaurant near Senflok, but they could not agree a time and a place to kill him. The main obstruction, according to Preucil, was his continuous fear of Gestapo surveillance and the fact that if they shot the two men, they would be detained by the attendant surveillance team.

The discussion moved on and Preucil added that he met with a man called Miroslav Hajek, whom he considered to be another Gestapo agent. He also believed Bohuslav Cadil in Mechenice to be a Gestapo man. Preucil claimed he was told by a Czech interpreter in the Prague Gestapo, that Cadil was working for them and had betrayed a Captain Miller. (I have been unable to confirm this man's identity. There was a British Secret Intelligence Service (SIS) officer called Major James Miller in the Balkans, but this does not appear to be a match.)

Preucil also told his interviewers, that he believed an ex-girlfriend named Ella Fortikova was probably an agent of the Gestapo.

On or about the 15 February 1943, Preucil claimed he was called in by the Gestapo. He was shown a photograph of Karel Kutlovas – an airman in England who Preucil denied knowing. Part of the image was covered by the Gestapo official, but when placed back on to the table, the other side of the photograph was revealed. The exposed portion showed another Czech airman, but Preucil did not know him. When the Gestapo saw him look at this second man, he was rebuked and Preucil told his Czech interrogators that he felt this man must have been another Gestapo agent, although no name was mentioned.

In his interviews, Preucil was at pains to reiterate that he had been called in by the Gestapo on numerous dates, but had never revealed anything to them. (Why they would give him a gun, a large financial reward and keep summoning him if he had given them nothing, presumably did not enter his mind.)

On another occasion at Karel Čurda's apartment, Preucil said he met two other men. The two men were introduced by Čurda as fellow parachutists (SOE agents). Their names were given as Kindl and Grabovsky and they admitted that they were now working for the Gestapo, although Preucil claimed he had told them not to do so. (Lieutenant Vaclav Kindl and Sergeant Bohuslav Grabovsky were part of the three-man Operation Intransitive SOE team dropped on 29/30 April 1942. They were to sabotage an oil installation at Kolin, but lost all their equipment and went into hiding. Kindl and Grabovsky were detained by the Gestapo and agreed to collaborate; however, Grabovsky failed to impress and was sent to Terezín concentration camp where he was executed in October 1944. Kindl continued to work with the Gestapo and was accidentally killed by gunfire on 20 May 1944.)

Preucil was now scattering information throughout his interviews, chopping and changing his accounts.

He soon moved back to the Gerik and Tomanova incident, stating that on 2 November 1943, he was summoned by the Gestapo and accused of tipping off the Tomanova family, and even of dating Milena Tomanova. They accused him of stating that Gerik was an agent and telling the family that the letter came from the Gestapo – (the Gestapo had actually been sending Gerik with these letters according to Preucil in his 13 June interrogation).

When the Gestapo had finished interrogating him, Preucil says he was bundled into a car and taken straight to Terezín concentration camp. He was imprisoned as a political prisoner with no further directions from the Gestapo, although they once asked him about fellow prisoner Dr Krajina.

On New Year's Eve 1943, Preucil claimed he was with other prisoners in the camp and one inmate named Josef Tuma was reciting a newspaper report about Hitler's recent speech. Tuma read it out aloud in a gloomy tone, while other detainees like Emil Lukes joined in with the comedy. Preucil claimed the guards must have heard their mockery and they beat the men before putting them all, including Preucil, in solitary confinement.

Preucil was at pains to point out to the Czech investigators, that he also informed fellow prisoner – Dr Vladimir Krajina, a friend of exiled President Eduard Benes – about Čurda and Gerik. He said they both agreed that whoever survived the camp, would ensure they were punished after the war. While in prison, Preucil claimed he was interrogated three times about the Tomanova family, but he did not expand upon this statement.

Eventually, on 3 May 1944, he said he was released from Terezín. The Gestapo, according to Preucil, did not impose any conditions upon him and he returned to his parents' home in Trebsin.

A short time later, the Gestapo came calling once more and they gave him a job in the Welfare Office at the Veletrzny Palace in Prague. Preucil claimed the Gestapo initially gave him no directions, but they later directed him to watch and report on General Engler in the office. Preucil added that he actually warned the old general of German intentions, while telling him about his own history and the Gestapo.

Preucil also claimed to have tipped off a man named Kratochvila, who was employed in the supply office in Karlin. With the help of his own cousin (Augustin Povolny), he claimed to have warned a third man called Kopecke, that he was being watched by the Gestapo.

Preucil told the Czech team that his own mother, Marie Preucil, was summoned by the Gestapo and directed to inform on her son – giving details of who visited him and where he went. The pressure caused her to become ill with stress and depression and she had to attend the Bulovka hospital in Prague.

Augustin Preucil clearly wanted the Czech authorities to believe he had been in a catch-22 situation and was actually a loyal patriot. He told the interviewers that he too suffered from constant tension due to the Gestapo pressure, and had to be placed sick in January 1945.

Preucil told his interrogators that in the summer of 1944, the Gestapo gave him a new task. A Polish male from Libno had informed them that a group of young people, led by a female called Petrina, wanted to flee to Slovakia and join an uprising there. Preucil by his own admission, went to an inn in Libno where he encountered this group of people. He spoke with Petrina about running away and joining the uprising, before he told the

Gestapo their intelligence was false. However, the Gestapo sent another agent called Darido to check this information and he, according to Preucil, took on the investigation. As far as Preucil knew, the group was later arrested and punished for running away from their compulsory work.

Preucil said he was also directed to investigate the case of Miroslav Hajek, but he did not give any details.

Preucil continued, telling the interviewers that by February 1945, he tried to avoid the Germans. He stayed away from his own apartment in case they arrested him and he stayed with his new girlfriend Jirina Vanisova in the Venkov district of Prague.

His new girlfriend had been 'approached' by a man called Preizeler on 29 January 1945. The man had sent her a letter asking for a date, saying he had seen her on the train between Prague and Zbraslav. Jirina had not used that train, so when she told Preucil of this man and the letter, he said he suspected Gestapo involvement, and another trick.

The Czech interrogators showed Preucil the letter, said to have been sent by Preizeler to Jirina Vanisova. Preucil examined the document and confirmed this was the actual letter.

Preucil was then asked about 1,500 Koruna worth of vouchers sent to Ella Fortikova, his ex-girlfriend. Preucil stated that she had been his girlfriend, and in his opinion, she had given information to the Gestapo about him. He claimed she pretended to be pregnant (intimating he was the father) and needed a nurse. She wanted money from him and he believed she was actually trying to identify if he was receiving money from England.

Preucil told the investigation team that from the 100,000 Koruna the Gestapo had given him in December 1941, he had given 38,000 Koruna in presents to Milena Tomanova. He spent 12,000 on entertainment and travel, leaving 50,000 for himself. In essence he was broke and had spent all the reward money.

Preucil stated that his friend Max Brantal had told him on the 6 January 1945, that the Gestapo suspected Preucil of collaborating with the Czech resistance movement. Brantal had been summoned and ordered by the Gestapo to watch Preucil and report everything to them.

When questioned about his ability with the German language, Preucil claimed he did not speak German. He was then shown a lined notebook seized by the Czech investigators. The pages were handwritten with Czech to German translations for numerous words. He soon admitted the words were in his own handwriting and had come from his time in Terezín concentration camp. In the camp he told his interviewers that the prisoners had been ordered to study from a book called '1,000 words of German'. Why he still had this notebook nearly two years later was not explained.

The interview was concluded and the Czech investigators returned to their research.

On 3 August 1945, Preucil gave a statement under caution. This was in response to information and statements the Czech investigators had received and served upon him. He stated,

> I don't feel guilty. I admit that I considered Cadil to be a Gestapo agent who was chasing me. I wanted to get rid of him and that is why I pointed out his contradictory anti-German statements to one of the Gestapo interpreters, but not to Josef Chalupský

who had actually warned me against Cadil. I know that Cadil was arrested, but I don't know why. I also considered Ladislav Skvor from Mechenice to be a tool of the Gestapo, which was watching and persecuting me. Skvor ran away from work in Risa and asked me to provide him with confirmation that he was employed.

In this, I saw an attempt by the Gestapo to convince me again of anti-German activity, and that is why I reported it to one of the Gestapo officials, saying that Ladislav Skvor was still harassing me. The Gestapo did not write any protocol with me, so I wasn't notified by hand, I didn't sign anything. I know that Skvor was arrested by the Gestapo, but I don't know if it happened as a result of me above report.

I thought that as an aviator I could get rid of people who would threaten me, so that after the war I could submit a report on the activities and the activities of other members of the Czech and foreign troops who somehow fell into the hands of the Germans. To Captain Ropeznik and Lt. Machalek in Agde (France), I stated that I had actually been sent by the Gestapo to Poland for spy on Czech soldiers.

(Lieutenant Machalek, was possibly Jiri Machacek, a Czech fighter pilot who escaped via Poland to France and attended the Hurricane course on No. 6 OTU like Preucil. He was killed in action in July 1941.)

After three months and a number of interrogations, it was clear that Augustin Preucil was trying to position himself as a patriot who got lost and sought to identify traitors such as Karel Čurda, Viliam Gerik and others after the war. The problem was, his accounts kept changing ever so slightly, and rather than give a full and detailed account as soon as possible, it was having to be drawn from him bit by bit.

On 16 August 1945, a further interview of Preucil took place. Unlike the earlier interview when he said he had not identified Karel or Miksovsky (the men at the restaurant who sent Czech airmen to Poland in 1939), this time he admitted that he had been beaten and threatened with the arrest of his own parents if he did not give information. Under this pressure, he told the Gestapo that Miksovsky arranged the passage of Czechoslovakian airmen to Poland, begging them not to harm him or his parents. The Gestapo agreed not to harm them if he worked for them in Poland, sending intelligence back about the airmen there. Preucil now admitted sending one report back to the contact called Smetana, and included in the report a plea for the Gestapo to leave the 'Wolf', meaning Miksovsky, until he returned to the Protectorate. However, the Gestapo had already detained Miksovsky. (Preucil had previously stated he had sent two messages back to Smetana Bedřich with no information contained in their text.)

Preucil could not control himself in his interviews and he went on to give further details of the Tomanova and Gerik incident. This time he admitted betraying the traitor Gerik to the Gestapo as he wanted to save the family from him. Preucil viewed Gerik as an agent provocateur who had already been rewarded for betraying the assassins of Reinhard Heydrich. Preucil said he had turned to the Gestapo interpreter Josef

Chalupský for assistance by intervening with the relevant Kommissar. The Kommissar was to be told that Gerik wanted to hand over this letter from an airman called Modrak in England, declaring himself to the family as a parachutist. Preucil believed Chalupský had intervened, but nothing happened.

With no apparent movement by the Gestapo, Preucil claimed he took Milena Tomanova to see Kommissar Leimer at the Petschek Palace in Prague. She told Leimer that Gerik had approached her with the letter. Preucil then added that Milena had previously told him that Gerik had been to see her in the autumn or winter of 1942, but when she told Leimer that Gerik had visited her in the spring of that year, he was shocked. (This would have been around the time Viliam Gerik had been dropped into the country and when he first met Augustin Preucil in Prague.)

Augustin Preucil was playing a very dangerous game and continued to present himself as the Czech patriot to the investigators. What he did not realise was that the investigation team were collecting statements from most of the people he was naming – and what they were telling the investigators was very different from Preucil's account.

A few days later, on 22 August 1945, Preucil's interrogation resumed. It appears the continued questioning was a tactic, not only did it mean he had to remember each element he had previously recounted, but it allowed the investigators to continually check each strand of his story.

Once again, Preucil returned to his time in England. He said he felt such mistrust from the RAF that he had the impression they believed he was a German spy. (It is a fact that the RAF and the British authorities in 1940/41 were concerned some of those joining from Czechoslovakia and Poland may have German or communist sympathies. As a result, the intelligence community were keen to check the backgrounds of the new arrivals and observe their behaviour. This meant interviews and close supervision, something the Eastern European arrivals must have thought odd.)

Preucil told his interrogators that he once violated the RAF regulations by performing low-level aerobatics. He then added that court martial proceedings 'should' have been initiated and he believed any court would hold the fact he had once been with the Gestapo as a negative point! Despite making this declaration, he never told the Czech investigators he had reported his time with the Prague Gestapo to anyone from the RAF. If he had, things might have ended differently.

The flight to Belgium was one he claimed not to have envisaged. He had accidently fired his Hurricane's machine guns in mock combat and with the perceived mistrust, he believed the RAF would not believe this to have been an innocent error. This in itself would lead to a court martial and for this reason, he decided to fly from England to Switzerland where he hoped to claim asylum. Preucil added that after the war that he wanted to return to Czechoslovakia to clear his name and explain the events. However, he ran out of fuel and made a forced landing in Belgium. (How a relatively experienced pilot had not considered the range and fuel capacity of the Hawker Hurricane was not apparently explained by Preucil or explored by the interviewing officers at the time.)

Up to this time, Preucil does not appear to have ever mentioned his involvement with the interrogation of Czechoslovakian (RAF Volunteer Reserve) aircrew in 1944 or any other time. However, in this latest interview, he stated that he saw Flight Lieutenant František Burda in the Gestapo building in Prague. Preucil claimed he had been summoned by the Gestapo and saw Burda sitting on a bench. He said he had given Burda a cigarette and wanted to talk, but a Gestapo officer quickly pulled Preucil away from him. (It is worth pointing out that the Gestapo building had offices on the upper floors, but the basement area was reserved for prisoners. It contained cells made from old bank vaults, a waiting area with plain white walls, bare wooden benches and interrogation rooms. It is likely Preucil had met Burda, just like Gerik and Čurda, in this waiting area where they had been sat on benches awaiting interrogation.)

This was as close as Preucil would get to talking about captured Czechoslovakian airmen and their interrogation, but as we shall see later, he was heavily involved in that aspect of Gestapo 'work'.

It appears from the court records, there were no more interrogations until the 8 January 1946 (or at least no documented interrogations). The Czech authorities were building a strong case against the rogue pilot who kept giving them conflicting information.

On the 8 January 1946, Preucil went back over his demobilisation from the air force in February 1939. He said he had returned to his parents farm at Trebsin and worked on the small holding. Clearly the interrogators were fine-checking his accounts.

He claimed to have been arrested by the Gestapo in July 1939, before going on to state once again that he had got lost in fog on 18 September 1941, and flown the Hurricane in a southerly direction, believing he was over England. When he ran out of 'gas', he made a forced landing, still thinking he was in England. In fact, it was Belgium and the local civilians gave him clothes. Preucil claimed a Polish man who was present went away and was not seen again – apparently trying to blame this man for his arrest by the Germans. (This contradicted his earlier interviews when he said a Belgian was responsible. In addition, the Belgian resistance report to British Intelligence had stated the local constable was responsible. Preucil was now even contradicting the reason for the flight and his fear of a court martial.)

It was clear to the Czechoslovakian authorities that not only was Augustin Preucil changing his accounts, but he was also a Gestapo agent.

Those involved with the pilot would certainly give a very different account of his behaviour and actions since 1939.

Chapter Three

Max Brantal
(Friend and close associate)

Max Brantal was one man the investigators were keen to trace and interview. A man Preucil had stated was a close friend, he was quickly located and interviewed by the Czech investigation team. He told them he had served with Augustin Preucil in the Czechoslovakian Air Force and knew him very well.

After they were demobilised in early 1939, Brantal went to work as an editor at the art school in Prague. He knew Preucil had also left the air force in February 1939 and gone back to Trebsin to live with his parents, but he remained in contact with him until the summer when Augustin suddenly disappeared.

A short time later, Brantal says he received a note from Preucil, who said he was in Poland. This was followed a short time later by a letter from France and Max knew his friend was with the armed forces in that country.

That was the last time he heard from Preucil until the end of 1941, when he heard through the proverbial grapevine that he had returned to Czechoslovakia. With the Nazis still in control of the country, Brantal could not believe this rumour, so he travelled to Trebsin where he found his old friend.

Brantal explained to the post-war investigators that Preucil told him he had escaped from the Germans in the summer of

1939. He then moved on to Poland, before going to France and finally England. He said he had been in training as a parachutist in England and received an order to fly a plane to Germany and land it there. Once in Germany he was to collect information for the English.

Preucil told Max Brantal that he landed the plane near Berlin where he was quickly detained. (Whether this was exactly what Preucil had told him or Brantal had been told he had been taken to Berlin and was confused is unknown.) Preucil told him that he was interrogated by the Germans, but he did not reveal anything as he had been trained for this in England. Eventually, they released him after nine days detention.

Brantal told the investigators that when Preucil returned in 1941, he had a scar over his eye and attributed this to his crash landing. When the two men met, Preucil told his old friend that he was still under the supervision of the Gestapo and was constantly under surveillance. He advised Brantal to be careful the Gestapo did not find out about their friendship.

Brantal was keen to tell the investigators he trusted Preucil implicitly as a Czech patriot. Preucil had also told him he had money which had been sent to him by the English.

The two men, despite Preucil's warnings, revived their old friendship and met regularly, sometimes at Augustin's apartment in Prague, which he had moved in to from Trebsin. (How he financed this apartment was clearly never discussed or considered.)

Max Brantal told the investigators that Preucil never spoke of working for the Gestapo, but that in time, he admitted that the Gestapo did give him certain tasks – although he claimed he never completed them.

About a month before the assassination of Reinhard Heydrich, Preucil told Brantal that a 'Large German animal would be shot within a month.' When Heydrich was assassinated, Preucil laughed about his correct prediction. Max Brantal explained to the investigators that he took Preucil's correct prediction as being due to his contact with England and another agent he claimed to know. As a result of this, Brantal had full confidence in Augustin Preucil.

Max Brantal explained that after the parachutists had been killed at the church in Resslova Street, Prague, Preucil informed him about Viliam Gerik and Karel Jerhot (Čurda). Preucil told Brantal that the two men were Czechoslovakian parachutists who had betrayed those in the church and now worked for the Gestapo. Preucil never explained to him how he knew this information, but he also told Brantal that the two men had shared the 10 million Koruna reward from the Germans. Preucil begged Brantal to ensure the two traitors were brought to justice, in the event he did not personally survive the war. Brantal swore he would do this.

Shortly after this, Preucil told Brantal that Jerhot's real name was in fact Karel Čurda and supplied his home address.

In the autumn of 1942, Brantal met an old friend called Milena Tomanova. She told him that a man called Malik had approached her father with a letter from Sergeant Modrak, a Czech aviator in England. This aviator was an admirer of Milena's sister, Irena. The man (actually called Gerik) told Milena's father that he was a stranded parachutist and needed support. Her father gave him some food stamps and sent him away. The man returned later and showed an identification card, explaining that he had received it from the Gestapo with whom he was now registered.

Brantal contacted Preucil and told him this story. Preucil arranged to meet with Milena Tomanova and told her he would speak with the Gestapo and get Modrak/Gerik away from her family. Preucil also told Max Brantal that he knew a Czech Gestapo agent called Chalupský or Chalpnicky and would speak with him.

Brantal explained that he was aware that Milena and her father – Karel Tomanova – were later sent to see the Gestapo and Gerik was arrested. Preucil had told Brantal that he had reported Gerik to the Gestapo, but did not explain how this was achieved.

According to Brantal, Preucil had called Čurda and Gerik traitors and said he wanted to 'remove them both'. Preucil talked about shooting them as soon as possible with a pistol he had been given by the Gestapo for self-defence, and he believed Preucil really intended to do this.

Brantal explained to the investigators that Preucil had introduced him to Karel Čurda in a beer hall near Senflok. They had talked about mundane matters before Brantal departed. Preucil later warned Brantal that Čurda was a traitor in the service of the Gestapo and it was good they had met, so he could report him to the authorities after the war's conclusion.

Brantal added that Preucil continued to talk about eliminating Gerik and Čurda and again asked him for assistance. He agreed to help kill them and Preucil said he would get him a pistol. However, despite Preucil's proclamations, no action was ever taken against the two men – at least not to Max Brantal's knowledge.

At the end of 1942, Max Brantal got a role at the Arts and Crafts school in Prague. There he met Miloslav Hajek during a visit from Augustin Preucil. The three men would often converse and Preucil and Hajek became very friendly, until a time when Brantal noticed the relationship between the two men had become strained.

It was clear to Brantal that they suspected one another of collaborating with the Gestapo. Preucil later told Brantal that he had seen Hajek at the Gestapo building and that he had discovered he was an agent. Brantal thought Hajek's behaviour at the school was odd, but could not give a specific example of him ever reporting anyone to the Gestapo. However, on the contrary, Hajek had warned Max Brantal that Preucil was a Gestapo agent and fraudster.

Brantal complicated things further by then stating that Hajek had been in an inn in Krizovnicke Street in Prague, when he admitted to Brantal that he was with the Gestapo. Brantal took this to mean he was working as an 'eye' for the Germans and in fact was against them i.e., in his position at the school, Hajek was expected to report persons to the Gestapo, but he was actually a Czech patriot.

In the autumn of 1943, Augustin Preucil disappeared again; he had been imprisoned in the concentration camp at Terezín. Preucil was released from Terezín in April 1944. Preucil went to see Brantal and told him that Miroslav Hajek had been to blame for his arrest and imprisonment. In addition, Preucil claimed that in Mechenice an innkeeper called Cadil and an Ella Fortikova were responsible for his arrest and were Gestapo 'aides'.

Preucil went back to live with his parents in Trebsin before moving to a new home in the Vela Market Palace.

Preucil told Brantal that since his arrest and imprisonment, the Gestapo no longer trusted him; but they soon asked for his cooperation again.

Brantal was at pains to explain that at the time, he trusted his friend implicitly, but he could never understand his link with the Gestapo. Preucil had explained that he was to observe Czechs on the orders of the Gestapo, but he never did this.

On another occasion, the two men got into discussion and Brantal pointed out that the Gestapo would want results for the money they gave him. (Clearly, he now knew the Gestapo were paying Preucil.) Preucil did not seem too concerned and told Brantal that he did things in such a way that 'bad people', such as black marketeers and German sympathisers in the councils, were reported by him to the Gestapo.

Preucil was desperate to get revenge against Miroslav Hajek. However, Brantal was not convinced of Hajek's guilt and warned him of Preucil's intentions. Hajek dismissed the threat from Preucil, telling Brantal he was not afraid of him.

On 14 December 1944, Preucil told Brantal that he was now a happy man, as Hajek had been arrested. Brantal asked if he was convinced that Hajek was a traitor and a Gestapo agent, but Preucil said that Brantal should not be too concerned. He knew what he was doing and he had acted correctly. He told Brantal that people like Hajek would betray their own people for just fifty Koruna and must be removed as traitors.

Brantal then admitted to the Czech investigators that he was unhappy with the influence the Gestapo clearly had over his old friend at the time. Brantal was summoned to give evidence to the Gestapo against Miloslav Hajek, and as he was not convinced about the man's guilt he asked for Preucil's advice. Preucil told him to just say Miroslav Hajek was a communist.

Brantal went to the Gestapo and was interrogated for three hours. They asked if Hajek was a communist, but he told them he did not know as Hajek had previously told him that he worked for the Gestapo. The Gestapo then started to quiz Brantal about Augustin Preucil. Brantal told the interrogating Gestapo Kommissar that Preucil was a Gestapo agent, but this was denied by the official. The Kommissar then asked Brantal if he knew the difference between being an agent and just working for the Gestapo.

The Kommissar demanded that Brantal work for them but he refused, saying he was a Czechoslovakian soldier and would not do this. As soon as he said this, the Kommissar became very angry and shouted threats and abuse at him. Eventually, the Gestapo official calmed down and directed Brantal to watch Preucil and report back to him every fourteen days. He was to observe and gather details of who Preucil met and where he went. He would be rewarded if he carried out this work, but he must never tell Preucil of this surveillance.

Despite the threats and directions, Brantal told the Czech investigators that he immediately informed Preucil of what the

Gestapo had ordered. Preucil thanked him for his honesty, but deep-down Max Brantal believed his old friend no longer trusted him.

The two men rarely saw one another after this, mainly because Preucil told him they should not see one another until after the war.

Brantal went to the Gestapo Kommissar and told him that he had not seen Preucil and therefore had nothing to report. He did not state the Gestapo man's reaction to this news.

After the war, Brantal met with Preucil in a restaurant in Spalena Street, Prague. The two men talked calmly about the German occupation and what had occurred, but Preucil told him not to worry, as he had been a Czech agent operating for England.

Brantal's evidence and statements portray a man who was possibly blinded by loyalty to a close friend. How, eight decades later, he could not see that Preucil was working for the Gestapo is unbelievable. At the very least, those who met and trusted Preucil, must have wondered how a man who had been so close to the Germans and served in the RAF in England, could wander around the Protectorate so freely. How could he be imprisoned at Terezín – allegedly as a suspected British agent – and then be allowed to go free and work for the Gestapo again?

It must have been infuriating for the Czech investigators that people like Max Brantal appeared to go along with Augustin Preucil's deception, or was Max Brantal playing a game with two faces just like his old friend?

It appears the Czechoslovakian authorities were unsure about the loyalty of Max Brantal in 1945 and 1946, but he managed to avoid the fate of a number of Czech traitors like Preucil, Gerik and Čurda.

What happened to Max Brantal in the following years is unclear.

The Czechoslovakian investigation team were now getting a clearer picture of Augustin Preucil's activities during the war and, more importantly to them, his activities in Prague.

Chapter Four

Karel Čurda and Viliam Gerik (SOE traitors)

Karel Čurda was one of three names on the most wanted list, once the Czech authorities returned to power. The others being Augustin Preucil and Viliam Gerik.

Čurda was quickly detained on 19 May 1945 and incarcerated in Pankrác Prison in Prague, some saying he accepted his fate without trying to flee. The reinstalled Czech authorities were only too aware of his treachery surrounding the assassination of Heydrich, but also the betrayal of other SOE agents such as František Pospisil. However, before justice could be served, they needed to obtain evidence from him about the treachery of other people – such as his associate, Augustin Preucil.

Čurda told the investigation team that he had been an SOE parachutist dropped into the country from England in March 1942. He was dropped in the area of Telc in Moravia, but he did not detail his operation and links with the other SOE parachutists.

Karel Čurda explained that he surrendered to the Gestapo in Prague in June 1942, where he was arrested and kept in custody for seven weeks before being freed. (He did not discuss in this interview why he had gone to the Gestapo or what he had told them – this was probably documented elsewhere for his own impending trial and the interrogators did not want him to give contradictory or varying information that could undermine his prosecution.)

He said he met Augustin Preucil in the summer of the same year. Čurda was in the Gestapo headquarters being questioned about the SOE training camps in the United Kingdom, when a man he did not recognise entered the room. This was Augustin Preucil.

Preucil did not want to enter the room and tried to turn back, but the Gestapo official told him, 'Don't be afraid, don't be shy, just go in.' Preucil gave Čurda some newspapers which contained a photograph of a Czechoslovakian airman. Preucil showed him the image of the Czech pilot and identified him as an airman who had shot down six or eight German aircraft. (Why he did this is not clear, was it an 'ice-breaker' or was he claiming to be the pilot?)

Čurda claimed that Viliam Gerik was also present, but he could not remember if Gerik spoke with Preucil that day. (At the time, Gerik was a free man, no longer detained by the Gestapo and apparently working for them.)

Čurda told the investigators that Preucil was apparently well informed about his position as a prisoner. Preucil asked him if there had been talk in England about a Czech pilot who had flown a new plane to the Germans. Čurda claimed he told Preucil he had not heard of such a thing, but in reality, he had. Another Czechoslovakian pilot in England told him that one of their pilots had taken a plane. At this point, the Gestapo interrupted their conversation and removed Preucil from the room.

The two men met later and Preucil told Čurda that he had been sent to Poland by the Gestapo. He was also allegedly told to move on to France or England. When he moved to England, Preucil said he was directed to bring a new type of aircraft back to Germany, but he believed the English suspected him of spying and did not trust him. Preucil claimed to have deduced this from the number of British intelligence service personnel who were constantly visiting his airfield.

Preucil told Čurda that he even suspected his new English wife of being a British agent, as she spoke to him in German, as if testing whether he knew the language. He also told Čurda that the English intelligence service had even searched his apartment and he feared he would be arrested. It was at this point he decided to flee England.

Preucil also told Čurda that at his home airfield he was not trusted with a new aircraft, but only an old flying school machine. However, with the assistance of a Polish officer whom he did not name, he obtained a new machine – he did not tell Čurda the type of aircraft.

Preucil said he went on a practice flight with a young Polish pilot above and in the clouds. He then fired his guns at the Polish pilot – he did not state whether this was a deliberate act, causing the Polish pilot to fly away.

Preucil headed south, having already broken his radio receiver. This, he told Čurda, was to stop radio calls and the English tracking him. He landed somewhere in Belgium or The Netherlands and the Germans quickly detained him. He was questioned and taken back to Prague where he was eventually released. He admitted to Čurda that he had been given a reward of 100,000 Koruna for bringing the aircraft back to the Germans and even claimed that he was supposed to be promoted to the rank of a Luftwaffe officer.

Čurda told the Czech investigators that Preucil was not satisfied with his reward. He probably knew from the Gestapo that Čurda had received 5 million Koruna for his work during the Heydrich assassination investigation and was unhappy with his earlier reward.

Preucil confessed to Čurda that he worked for the Gestapo. On one occasion he told Čurda he was going to Dejvis to see a 'wild girl', and that Viliam Gerik had also been to see this girl. This, he claimed, was because Gerik wanted to hide 700,000 Koruna. Gerik had invited the girl to Brno, but he never told Preucil why he had done this.

Čurda told the investigators that Preucil 'somehow worked for the Gestapo', and had spent a lot of the reward money he had been given. At one stage, Preucil had mentioned the figure of about 30,000 Koruna being spent (or left) from the reward.

Karel Čurda fully admitted working for the Gestapo after going to them in June 1942. He knew a man called Diabo (almost certainly Heinz Diabo, Chief of Criminal section Prague Gestapo, and a colleague of Heinz Pannwitz and Oskar Fleischer). Diabo was introduced to Preucil by Čurda, but he already knew him from his visits to the Gestapo headquarters.

Karel Čurda admitted knowing and inviting two other parachutists from England to his apartment. Their names were Kindl and Grabovsky, and they went on to work for the Gestapo.

Kindl had already had a meeting with Augustin Preucil in a nearby restaurant. After the meeting, Preucil had attended the apartment of Čurda and wrote notes on two pieces of paper. It contained everything he had learnt from his meeting with Kindl and apparently Grabovsky. Preucil told Čurda that both men were drunk and they had told him everything he wanted to hear from the two ex-SOE agents. Preucil wanted Čurda to translate the notes into German for the Gestapo. Čurda did as he was asked and when Heinz Diabo of the Gestapo arrived, he was present when Preucil told the official about the two ex-SOE men. Diabo made notes of his own and a short time later, Grabovsky was arrested and imprisoned in Pankrác Prison. Kindl, as far as Čurda knew, was shot and killed during a later Gestapo operation while working with the Germans.

(Lieutenant Vaclav Kindl had continued to work with the Gestapo and was accidentally hit by gun fire and killed on 20 May 1944. Sergeant Bohuslav Grabovsky failed to impress the Gestapo and was eventually sent to Terezín concentration camp where he was executed in October 1944.)

Čurda said he remembered Preucil mentioning the fact that Čurda had been given pseudonym Karel Jerhot by the Gestapo. Preucil stated that he too wished to have a false identity, claiming that he had been the person who advised the Gestapo to give the former SOE man his cover name when he was released from the headquarters building.

Čurda impressed upon the interviewers that he only knew Preucil after being interrogated by the Gestapo in 1942. He did not know him in Britain, he did not work with him for the Gestapo and could not say for certain if Preucil actually worked for the Germans. He did not offer any more information to the investigating team. It appears he was awaiting trial and did not want to incriminate himself any further. There may also have been legal constraints which meant the investigators could not push the issue too far.

However, this limited evidence from Karel Čurda confirmed the links with Viliam Gerik, Grabovsky, Kindl and a number of Gestapo officers in Prague and the surrounding areas.

On this evidence alone, it now looked like Preucil may have been responsible for the eventual death of Bohuslav Grabovsky in Terezín concentration camp.

The other ex-SOE traitor, Viliam Gerik, was also detained after the end of the war. He had worked for the Gestapo but had been denounced by Augustin Preucil and arrested over the Tomanova affair. Sent to Pankrác Prison on the 6 April 1943, he was sent on to Terezín concentration camp and then to the infamous Dachau concentration camp. On 29 April 1945 he was liberated by the advancing US Army, but returned to Prague to be arrested within days and put on trial for his treachery.

Viliam Gerik was not as talkative as Karel Čurda and may have been confused or angry about the situation in which he now found himself. He had assisted the Gestapo, but was apparently betrayed and imprisoned in a concentration camp. He probably thought he would be considered a victim of the Nazi regime, not a tool of the Gestapo.

When interviewed by the Czech investigators, Gerik admitted being an SOE parachutist who was dropped into Slovakia on 27 March 1942. He lost his team and, unable to hold out any longer, he made his way to Prague where he handed himself in to the local police. Unfortunately, they handed him over to the Gestapo.

In April 1942, he was held at the Gestapo headquarters in Prague when he noticed Augustin Preucil in an adjacent room. Gerik was unsure whether the Gestapo had put Preucil in the room, or whether he had made his own way in to it.

Gestapo Inspector Oskar Fleischer asked Gerik if he knew Preucil. He told Gerik this was the man who had flown an aeroplane to them from England. The two men were left alone in the room and Preucil told Gerik that he had flown a Hurricane aircraft from England to the Continent. Gerik did not go into further detail with the investigators and it does not look as if they pushed the issue, rather like their interrogation of Čurda. (It is possible Čurda and Gerik had given more details which were not recorded.)

About two to three weeks later, Gerik says he saw Preucil again in the Gestapo building in Prague. Preucil again said he had been a pilot and served in England where he married an English woman. He bragged to Gerik that he used to work for the Gestapo, but he did not explain this comment or why he had come back to Czechoslovakia.

Viliam Gerik said he was interrogated and eventually released from prison and given various tasks by the Gestapo. Some weeks later he met Preucil again in Prague, but he claimed they did not speak to one another. The next time he saw Preucil was after the war and they had both been arrested.

Gerik added that Preucil had told him at one point that he had received 100,000 Koruna from the Gestapo, although he never explained why he received it. Gerik denied knowing anything about Preucil's activities in Prague, but he did remember him once saying he wanted to buy a car and should get the money from the Gestapo.

Gerik did not mention the issue with Milena Tomanova and her family and it does not appear the investigators wished to pursue that matter. Again, this may have been due to legal constraints as Gerik was also under investigation, and in time, he would also face a trial.

Although Czechoslovakian law was different to English and Scottish law, all legal systems apart from those in dictatorial states have issues with using the evidence of co-defendants against another accused.

In this case, the reinstalled Czechoslovakian authorities were trying to reimpose a fair legal system, while dealing with their three most wanted traitors. So many Czech citizens had died or been tortured and punished at the hands of the Nazi occupiers, that justice had to be seen to be done.

In many respects, the authorities already knew the three men had worked for the Gestapo, they would face justice in time, but they had to be seen to gather the necessary evidence, even if that came from the lips of the three men themselves. However, there were plenty of other witnesses to the activities of Augustin Preucil and his fellow traitors.

Chapter Five

Josef Chalupský
(Gestapo interpreter)

Josef Chalupský was a 41-year-old former Czech Police Officer in 1942. He worked for the Gestapo as an interpreter and had extensive contact and knowledge of Augustin Preucil. He was granted German citizenship and after the war became a StB agent in Czechoslovakia. It has been claimed that Chalupský interrogated the SOE parachutist František Pavelka (from the Operation Percentage team) and took part in the Resslova Street Church operations after Heydrich's assassination.

Chalupský was initially detained in May 1945 as a Gestapo official. He gave extensive details to the investigation team and appears to have been keen to assist them – possibly fearing for his own life at the time.

Josef Chalupský explained that the SBF, or the Sabotage-Fallschrimjager department (Sabotage and Parachutist department of the Gestapo), had a number of confidants who were former parachutists themselves or partisans. They were controlled by Kommissar Leimer and Jaroslav Nachtmann, who met them in several Gestapo-controlled apartments around Prague, many of which had been seized from prisoners.

Chalupský was aware that in June or July 1939, Inspectors Oskar Fleischer and Karel Hershelmann had sent a Czechoslovakian airman to Poland. His purpose was to join the Czech Legion and send information back to the Gestapo in Prague.

The former Gestapo man explained that the information was to be sent by mail to a dental assistant called František Smetana in Prague. (Preucil had called him 'Bedřich Smetana', possibly confusing him with the name of the composer, but František Smetana was a also a renowned cellist.)

Josef Chalupský explained that Smetana did not know anything about this at the time. The Gestapo approached Smetana and told him he would receive letters from abroad, as such he now worked for Fleischer, Herschelmann and the Gestapo. In addition, Smetana and his family were forced to take state citizenship and threatened with deportation to a concentration camp by Karel Herschelmann. Having no choice, Smetana became the conduit between Preucil and the Gestapo in Prague.

Chalupský soon discovered that in 1939, Oskar Fleischer had taken Gustav Preucil (NB: he did not call him Augustin), to the Polish border where he was allowed to cross into Poland. Preucil, he recalled, later made his way via France to England where he became a flying instructor for Polish pilots in the RAF.

One day Oskar Fleischer brought a letter from Preucil into the office. It had been sent from Paris. Fleischer handed the note to Chalupský to translate, as it was written in Czechoslovakian. According to Chalupský, the note was actually incomprehensible and rambling, talking about a dog or a wolf. (Was this the message Preucil had told his Czech interrogators he had sent from Poland, asking the Gestapo not to deal with the Wolf i.e., Miksovsky?)

Josef Chalupský said that in 1940 he overheard a conversation between Oskar Fleischer and Karel Herschelmann. They protested that 'the guy' didn't write to them, but later Fleischer arrived in the office with a letter from Paris which he showed to Herschelmann. Chalupský apparently believed that this was information from Preucil, who was now based at Chartres airfield, but this cannot be confirmed and it did not appear to be checked by the post-war Czech investigation team.

One day a telegram arrived at the Gestapo headquarters in Prague. It was sent from the German military authorities in France or Belgium. It stated that an English aviator named Preucil had landed there and claimed to be working for Oskar Fleischer. The local population, believing he was English, dressed him in civilian clothes, but he had the Germans arrest him and declared himself to be a Gestapo agent.

Chalupský told the investigators that Fleischer and Herschelmann rejoiced upon hearing this news and sent Chalupský as an interpreter with Gestapo Secretary Klaus Petereit to Berlin to bring Preucil back home to Prague.

According to Chalupský, when they arrived in Berlin, they found Preucil to have a slight injury to his face from his forced landing. He had been taken to the Luftwaffe headquarters in Berlin from Brussels, wearing his RAF sergeant's uniform. Preucil had drawn various maps and plans of military targets in Britain for the Luftwaffe, while giving them information about RAF airfields, warehouses (possibly the maintenance units he served at?) and warship anchorages. This information was all plotted on a detailed map by the Luftwaffe staff.

Josef Chalupský (Gestapo interpreter)

Preucil was mostly speaking in English when Chalupský arrived in Berlin, so he was not required for his Czech interpreting skills. He told the Czech investigators that he did not see the Hurricane flown by Preucil to Belgium, but that the Gestapo continually stated it was a brand-new aeroplane and they were very happy about this.

Preucil was conveyed by Chalupský and Petereit to Prague and interrogated further by the Gestapo, particularly by his agent controller – Oskar Fleischer. According to Chalupský, Preucil helpfully gave them all the names he could remember of the Czech airmen in France and England, using an official photograph album to do this. The album had been supplied by the Prague branch of the Abwehr (German military intelligence). One name supplied by Preucil was that of Krometo.

Preucil told them about morale and conditions for the Czechoslovakian airmen in England, and probably told them how suspicious the British were of their new allies.

Chalupský claimed that Preucil was rewarded with a sum of 100,000 Koruna (10,000 Reichsmarks) and he made a long and detailed agreement with Oskar Fleischer to work for the Gestapo in Prague. (This would normally be a signed agreement, but this, unlike a later 1944 version, was never recovered by the Czech investigation team.)

Although Oskar Fleischer was originally in charge of Preucil, Karel Herschelmann was in charge of the Czech Legion issue before it was passed on to Secretary Bauer. Preucil then became Bauer's confidant. (This was Gestapo Chief Secretary Bedřich Bauer.)

Despite the Gestapo clearly valuing their star agent, Josef Chalupský was keen to give his own opinion to the Czech investigators, stating that he thought 'Preucil was too stupid for the job'.

In 1943, the Gestapo closed Preucil down because he had told someone that he was a parachutist from England. (This could have been any one of a number of people including Milena Tomanova.) As a result, he was sent to Terezín concentration camp for about half a year.

Chalupský stated that in his opinion, he believed Preucil had been sent to spy on the other inmates because when he returned home, he looked very fit and healthy! Chalupský was uncertain about whether Augustin Preucil continued to work for the Gestapo after his release in 1944, this was because he was transferred to another department; but he considered it very likely as he always needed money.

Chalupský remembered that Preucil was in contact with the ex-SOE agents Karel Čurda and Viliam Gerik. Preucil had met them both at the Gestapo headquarters in Prague where Gerik drew plans of military targets in England and a plan of the school where the parachutists had been trained (almost certainly the Czech SOE training area around Arisaig and Morar in Scotland).

Chalupský also remembered Preucil being keen to draw his attention to Gerik. Preucil claimed that Gerik was probably working against the Germans and had kept quiet about a letter he was carrying from a Czech aviator in England. This was for a wine merchant's family in Dejvice. Chalupský recalled the family name had been Tomanova.

Josef Chalupský (Gestapo interpreter) 75

Chalupský recalled that Preucil was always trying to get Viliam Gerik to testify about anti-German activities. When he failed to do so, Preucil wanted Chalupský to report Gerik to Kommissar Leimer or Inspector Oskar Fleischer for being unsupportive of the Protectorate.

With regard to the wine merchant's family in Dejvice, Preucil had arranged for the daughter to be shown a series of photographs so that she could recognise and identify Viliam Gerik. Chalupský went with Preucil and handled the images which were supplied by Preucil himself. Chalupský thought the girl had identified Gerik, but he was not certain of this when he spoke to the investigators after the war.

Chalupský said he did report Gerik to the Gestapo as Preucil wished. When nothing happened to Gerik, Preucil brought the girl to the headquarters building and 'begged' Chalupský to plead with the Gestapo that nothing would happen to this girl and her family. Chalupský claimed he promised to do this and ensured that as, he called her, 'this prostitute' and her family would not be punished for the belated reporting of Viliam Gerik and the letter from England.

Chalupský continued, stating that he asked Kommissar Leimer not to write a report against the girl and her family in Dejvice. As far as he knew, nothing ever happened to the Tomanova family.

Josef Chalupský recounted to the investigators that Gestapo Kriminal Offizier Schultze was also involved, but he did not state exactly how he was involved in this issue. (Wilhelm Schultze was Chief of the 3rd Section of Prague Gestapo from 1941. He is believed by some to have actually been working for the British secret service although this has not been confirmed.)

The Gestapo did nothing about Gerik at first, so Preucil took the girl (Milena Tomanova) himself to see Kommissar Leimer. Chalupský said he did not know what was discussed or decided, but a few months later Gerik was arrested and imprisoned after the Gestapo set a trap for him. Chalupský added that he did not know why Preucil was always so keen to hand Viliam Gerik over to the Gestapo.

Josef Chalupský also recalled Preucil investigating others in the department in which he worked. He used another photograph album, loaned from the Abwehr (German Military Intelligence.) The album and its associated personnel files were held by Jiri Pitter, a Gestapo auxiliary and interpreter who worked for Chief Secretary Bedřich Bauer collating files.

The evidence of Josef Chalupský had knitted together many of the facts the investigators had already learned from Preucil and others. It was clear Augustin Preucil was being very economical with the truth, but the depth of his treachery was still to be discovered. Although the main Gestapo officers such as Fleischer, Bauer and Herschelmann were unaccounted for, there were a number of other Gestapo officials, interpreters and drivers who had been located. These men would also give statements to the investigation team about Augustin Preucil's activities in Czechoslovakia.

Chapter Six

Other Gestapo-linked witnesses

Hugo Heller

Hugo Heller told his Czech interviewers that he had been a teacher in Subusina near Litomerice in 1940. When the war started, however, he was redeployed to Germany, being assigned to the Gestapo in Prague as a driver and an interpreter. Heller's knowledge of the local roads was poor and it proved to be a handicap for his driving work, so he ended up being used as a Gestapo office assistant.

Heller told the Czech investigators that in 1941, he was in the apartment of Gestapo Kriminal Agent Handler Vilibalda Burgeho (sometimes known as Bunge) in Prague. Heller, being an ex-school teacher, tutored and looked after the Gestapo man's children.

One day Burgeho/Bunge was drunk and pointed out a man. Burgeho told Heller this man was a Czech, who had served in the Czechoslovakian Air Force in England and flown the latest type of British aircraft back to the Germans who learnt a lot about it. Burgeho claimed the matter had been discussed at the highest levels in Berlin, but now the man was his best confidant and agent in Prague. Heller later discovered the man's name to be Augustin Preucil.

Hugo Heller spoke freely with the investigation team and was keen to add that Gestapo confidants were paid financial rewards.

After he was told about Preucil by Burgeho, Heller said he paid more attention to Preucil's activities. He had seen Preucil at the Petschek Palace in Prague and knew he had attended the office of Vilibalda Burgeho, but he was never present for any of their meetings.

The last time he could recall seeing Preucil was in November 1944, outside the Petschek Palace. Preucil spoke with Heller and told him he had been imprisoned in Terezín for some 'stupid things', but he did not elaborate upon this.

On 5 or 6 December 1944, Heller said he was transferred to the Gestapo office in Benešov, where he worked as a clerical assistant. One day, he received an order from Kriminal Secretary Steinwardt (sometimes named Stainbart) to give the Chetnik station in Zbraslav a telephone order. They were to arrest an inn-keeper called Bohuslav Cadil in Mechenice. Cadil was duly arrested and brought into the Gestapo office; a few days later, Professor Josef Hurt, also of Mechenice, was arrested on the orders of Steinwardt. Heller recalled the two arrests being linked and constituting one prosecution case.

Despite being a clerical assistant, Hugo Heller was given the task of interrogating the two men on suspicion of spreading 'false news' from foreign radio broadcasts and spreading the word that Germany was the enemy. The two suspects' case file contained information signed by someone using the cipher 'Josef'.

Kriminal Secretary Steinwardt had asked Heller if he knew the agent using the name 'Josef'; he did not.

Later, on a business trip to Prague, Heller discovered that the agent called 'Josef' was actually Augustin Preucil and that he had supplied the information leading to the arrests of Bohuslav Cadil and Josef Hurt.

Heller told the Czech investigators that he was quite surprised at the time, that Preucil was still working for the Gestapo when the outcome of the war was already clear to all. Heller, clearly trying to endear himself to the Czech investigators, claimed to have allowed Josef Hurt to meet his wife while in custody, without the knowledge of the Gestapo officers.

Heller also stated that Professor Josef Hurt asked him who had reported him to the Gestapo. This was because Preucil was the only person he had discussed the radio issues with and he clearly suspected him of being the informant. Once the investigation was complete, Hurt and Cadil were transported to Terezín concentration camp. It was clear the primary evidence had come from Preucil.

Hugo Heller could give no further information about Augustin Preucil, but he remembered that another Gestapo official named Oswald Marx had been involved in the case of Hurt and Cadil in Benešov.

Oswald Marx

Oswald Marx was arrested after the war and interviewed by the Preucil investigation team. He had been employed as a driver for the Post Office in Rissa at the start of the war, but in August 1941, he was assigned to the Gestapo as a driver and Czech interpreter.

Marx worked at their headquarters in Prague at the Petschek Palace and by the summer of 1942, he was trusted enough to be allowed to work independently. He would report matters of people allegedly listening to foreign radio stations and then disseminating 'false news' to the wider Czech community.

Marx said he had served in Prague until the 4 April 1943, when he was transferred to the office in Benešov, where he performed the same role. He told the investigators that he did not personally know Augustin Preucil and he had never seen him at the Petschek Palace.

Marx knew that Preucil had been to see Hugo Heller, but he did not know why. He explained that his office was in another part of the building at the Gestapo headquarters, hence he did not see Preucil when he attended Prague.

His recollections of Preucil were somewhat vague, but when he was working in Benešov, Marx remembered either handling a report, or something similar, signed by Preucil.

The investigators asked Marx specifically, if he had seen Professor Josef Hurt, Ladislav Skvor or Bohuslav Cadil in the Benešov Gestapo offices. Marx claimed he could not confirm seeing them or their files and Hugo Heller never mentioned them to him. Marx was keen to point out that although he did handle political prisoner and suspect files, there were a great many of them and he did not recall seeing those belonging to these three men. He also added that Hugo Heller would accompany any prisoner transports to Terezín concentration camp.

Josef Eska

Josef Eska was a Gestapo Kriminal assistant officer in Prague. He gave evidence to the Czech investigators that he knew about

Augustin Preucil and that he had been sent by the Gestapo to England, before fleeing with an aeroplane back to Belgium with photographs for the Gestapo in Prague.

Augustin Preucil had been imprisoned in Terezín concentration camp, apparently for the purpose of gaining the trust of the high-profile prisoner – Dr Vladimir Krajina. Preucil had engaged the prisoner in conversation and tried to elicit information, but Krajina quickly realised Preucil knew facts only the Gestapo could have known. Krajina, therefore, suspected Preucil as being a Gestapo agent and tried to avoid him.

Eska told the interviewers that Preucil was also in contact with a fellow prisoner called Emil Lukes from Rosensko. Lukes told Preucil about a secret letter from General Ingra which Dr Krajina possessed. Preucil also learnt information from the camp barber – a man called Holic. When Preucil passed this information on to the Gestapo, Josef Eska claimed the camp barber was executed.

Eska also claimed that Preucil was released from Terezín for giving information about his fellow prisoners. He then added that Preucil 'somehow worked for the Czechs' towards the end of the war, but this comment was not developed further by the investigators. (This is worth remembering, as later in the book there are claims Preucil was working against the Nazis at the end of the war.)

Bohuslav David

The investigators sought another Gestapo official identified by Preucil and called David. Initially they located a Czech police

Kriminal Inspector called Jan David, but he claimed he did not know Augustin Preucil and had never been a member of the Gestapo. However, his brother, Bohuslav David, had been a member.

When located, Bohuslav David told the interviewing officers that on 15 March 1939 he had been a criminal police assistant in Graz. When the Germans occupied the country he remained in post, and on 20 December 1943 he was assigned to the Gestapo in Prague. Initially, he was entrusted with minor tasks like finding addresses, searching files or acting as an interpreter.

The first time he heard the name of Augustin Preucil was at the beginning of 1944, when it was announced that he (Preucil) was no longer in the Gestapo workforce and was in Terezín concentration camp.

Bohuslav David moved on to work in the department prosecuting persons for violating their work obligations and it occurred to him that Preucil had never been prosecuted for having no employment. (All fit and able-bodied people were required to work for the greater good of the Protectorate, failure to do so meant imprisonment.)

In the summer of 1944, David met Preucil after being assigned to assist him investigate a case. The investigation concerned a worker called Petrina, and some of her colleagues who allegedly wanted to flee to Slovakia and take part in an uprising. When he was assigned to Preucil, the Gestapo only mentioned the issue of running away from work and nothing was said about an uprising. David told the Czech investigators that Preucil was the one who mentioned fleeing to Slovakia and an uprising, not the Gestapo.

Bohuslav David says he went with Preucil to an inn called 'Na ruska' in Libno. Once inside the inn, David spoke with the inn-keeper and an elderly person, while Preucil was with the young people and Petrina in another room.

On the journey back, Preucil told David that the young people were poor and had run away from work in Risa. David asked why he was so interested in these people and Preucil replied that they were suspected of wanting to escape to Slovakia. Preucil never explained how he came to such a conclusion.

As a result of this, all those persons present in the inn were detained. Some were later released, but a number were punished for offences of not fulfilling their work duties. Preucil later told David, that the initial information had come from a Pole involved in the black-market, although he had no idea whether the Pole had been reported as well.

David told the Czech interviewers that Preucil was always talkative, but always careful with what he disclosed. He did not know anything else about Preucil's Gestapo activities and the last time he saw him was in front of the Gestapo building in Breddovsak Street.

David concluded his interview by stating that he had not been on duty since 2 March 1945 due to sickness. He therefore could not tell the investigators when Preucil stopped working for the Gestapo.

Although these men were lower-level employees of the Gestapo in Prague and Benešov, it was clear that they all knew Augustin Preucil was a Gestapo agent and involved in the arrests – and ultimately the deaths – of a number of people. It also appears that on many occasions his information was not corroborated and we can assume that Preucil was financially rewarded by the Gestapo for these actions. The evidence of those victims who were still alive was now an important part of the investigation and needed to be gathered as soon as possible.

Jiri Pitter

Jiri Pitter worked as a Gestapo clerk and told the investigators that he first saw Augustin Preucil in Prague, when he was a Gestapo informant.

Pitter said Preucil had been employed by Inspector Oskar Fleischer to go to Poland for fourteen days and report on the Czech Legion in 1939, but he did not return. In 1941, Preucil returned to Prague and agreed upon release to be a Gestapo confidant.

Pitter could not add very much, but he did remember that Preucil had followed a group of people who wanted to go to Slovakia to join the partisans (Petrina and the other workers). Someone called 'Apson' had reported this to the Gestapo and the group were detained in Prague – there were between six and ten of them. This, as far as Pitter could remember, was in 1944.

He recalled that in 1943, Preucil was arrested by the Gestapo and imprisoned at Terezín for about six months. After that he was released in 1944, but he again worked for the Gestapo.

Pitter claimed that Preucil informed Bedřich Bauer about a Czech pilot in England and a relative in the Czech Legion and this came from a photograph that was at Preucil's disposal. (Pitter did not mention their names.) This information was passed on to Jiri Pitter and he created a file from this information for the Gestapo records. He added that Preucil had always been helpful to him, but he could not add anything further about the Czech traitors activities.

SNB Station Commander Ludvík Němec

Ludvík Němec was one of the last people to apparently give evidence to the Czech investigators. He was in charge of the local police station covering the small town of Trebsin where Preucil's parents resided, and where he went following his release from Gestapo custody in late 1941.

Although Ludvík Němec was not a Gestapo officer or official, he was connected through his police work and so has been included in this section.

Němec told the investigators that after the Germans had occupied the border area, Augustin Preucil, who lived in Trebsin, applied for a travel permit to go to France and perhaps other countries (this was in 1938 or 1939). The local police station recommended that Preucil be issued with such a pass, but the German authorities refused.

A short time later (Němec said he couldn't remember if it was after the establishment of the so-called Protectorate or before) Augustin Preucil disappeared from the area. He said the rumour among the local population was that he had gone abroad illegally without official permission.

Out of prudence, Ludvík Němec said, 'He did not ask or look for anything to do with this allegation.' He did not even speak with Preucil's parents because according to regulations at the time, it would have been his duty to report the matter to the

Gestapo. This, in turn, would have exposed Preucil's parents to arrest and transportation to a concentration camp. No one ever asked about Augustin Preucil and so he left the matter alone.

In the autumn of 1941, Augustin Preucil suddenly returned to Trebsin and his parents' home address. Němec could not remember if his arrival had been communicated to the local police confidentially (by the Gestapo), or whether one of his subordinates had discovered this on one of their patrols. However, the local population were gossiping about Preucil's return and on 6 October 1941, Staff Inspector Vaclav Vaneta and Inspector František Vnouck had occasion to stop and question Augustin Preucil. They asked him where he had been staying and where he had returned from. Preucil told them he had been abroad and investigated by the Gestapo in Prague, before being released back to his parents' home.

Preucil told the two police officers that he had been told not to answer any local police questions and the police were not to question him. The two officers reported back to Němec. The station commander and his men were concerned that this was a test of their loyalty, so as a precaution, they reported the circumstances surrounding Preucil's return to the Gestapo in Prague. They asked whether they should detain Augustin Preucil or leave him alone. A short time afterwards, Němec received a phone call from a Gestapo man, who confirmed he was from the Prague Gestapo by giving the phone number as 10981. He confirmed that the Gestapo had been investigating Preucil and directed Němec to have Preucil report to the Gestapo headquarters in Prague – in office CIS.612, at 10.00 hours the next morning (7 October 1941). The message was duly delivered by a local police officer to Preucil, but Němec did not get a fuller explanation. He knew he should leave the matter with the Gestapo for his own safety.

Němec spoke with Augustin Preucil a number of times after this date, usually at the Chancellery in Trebsin. He said he carefully asked Preucil about why he was abroad and his experiences. Preucil told him that after the Germans had occupied France, he did not feel safe anymore and that's why he tried to get back to his homeland illegally. Němec said he could not remember, over five years later, whether Preucil said he had crossed the Swiss border, or the border from Switzerland to Germany, where he was detained and handed over to the Gestapo in Prague.

Preucil had told Němec he had been tortured by the Gestapo and showed him a scar above his eye (clearly the injury from his forced landing and not due to torture).

Němec had continued to casually question him as he knew the Gestapo would not release a suspect under investigation, and certainly not one who had returned from another country. Němec and the other local police officers did not trust Preucil and were very wary of him, but they were more concerned about the Gestapo.

Preucil told the Police Station Commander that he had married an English woman he had met while in France, leaving her there. Němec knew Preucil had been a pilot before the war and asked him about flying and aviation abroad, but he was evasive and did not say anything. After some weeks or months, Preucil seemed to be moving freely around the local community; he frequented local inns in Trebsin, especially that run by František Jaruska.

Němec recalled that by 1942 Preucil did not seem to have any employment and this made the police officers suspect him even more.

In May and June 1942, during the assassination of Reinhard Heydrich and the subsequent investigations, Preucil was not in the Trebsin area and the local police did not know where he was.

In the autumn of 1942, the village of Trebsin and the surrounding area was displaced for the creation of an SS training camp. The Preucil family home, like many others, was removed and they went to Mechenice. After the family left Trebsin, Němec said neither he or his officers had seen or spoken to Preucil.

Němec added that he had known Augustin Preucil since his childhood. He recalled that the young Preucil was not very diligent and a bit of a mother's boy, while his father was quite strict with him. As a boy, his parents bought him a bike with a motor, as well as a typewriter. Augustin was sent on a business course in Prague before eventually going to the flying school and then joining the military training school at Prostejov.

On first appearances this evidence does not seem to be too damning, but it is clear the local police officers suspected Preucil was working for the Gestapo. It also shows how fearful the Czech police were of the Gestapo. They were, to a degree, more concerned with preserving their own lives than questioning the integrity and actions of Preucil.

Chapter Seven

The Terezín prisoners

The Czech investigation team was keen to obtain evidence from the prisoners who had been incarcerated with Augustin Preucil in Terezín concentration camp. They had heard a number of stories, but they needed to hear this from the prisoners themselves – if they had survived.

Alois Kolomaznik

Alois Kolomaznik had been incarcerated in Terezín, but the reasons for his imprisonment are unknown. He told the investigators that he remembered Augustin Preucil arriving at the prison and joining their cell, number 101, about a year before he was interviewed as a witness (early-mid 1944?).

Kolomaznik recalled Preucil being talkative, but sometimes he 'sounded off' and was very vocal. For example, he once stated that everything was fine and the Germans would lose the war and go home, but when Kolomaznik told him he was talking nonsense, Preucil denied ever making such positive statements.

One day, Preucil went to the cell toilet (not a pleasant location in Terezín with no running water). He said he wanted to stick his toothbrush in the excrement and clean his teeth with it. The other inmates told him to stop this erratic, odd behaviour, but Preucil did not believe he had ever done such things. His behaviour seems to perhaps be, in modern parlance, comparable with bipolar disorder.

Kolomaznik added that Preucil also fiddled with the door handle and pretended to be listening to a radio, claiming it was faulty. He then demanded that another prisoner, called Brejcha, fix it for him.

Preucil told Kolomaznik that he would cook like a cook, while Kolomaznik went to court. He also added that he would fight with Brejcha in the cell toilet (the same prisoner whom he wanted to 'fix the radio'). Kolomaznik recalled that Brejcha was afraid of Preucil because he was smaller and much weaker than him.

Kolomaznik thought Preucil 'had something wrong with his head', because he had stated he had been in three plane crashes. Preucil also told Kolomaznik that he had been poisoned by cigarettes given to him by the Gestapo.

Alois Kolomaznik clearly thought Preucil was unstable and told the investigators that he regularly spoke complete nonsense.

Kolomaznik appears to have been the only witness to have claimed Preucil was unstable. Was this part of an act? What did the other Terezín inmates think of Augustin Preucil?

Dr Vladimir Krajina

Dr Krajina was a university professor and political prisoner. He was the only member of the UVOD (resistance group) not to be identified and captured or killed during the clampdown after Reinhard Heydrich's death in 1942. He managed to continue contacting SOE parachutists while sending radio messages back to London, but in February 1943, he was arrested and sent to Terezín as a so-called 'special prisoner'. This meant he required close supervision at all times.

Augustin Preucil claimed in his interrogation to have told Krajina about Čurda and Gerik and the need to bring them to justice. Josef Eska, a Gestapo Kriminal Assistant, had already told the Czech investigators that Preucil had been imprisoned in Terezín for the purpose of gaining the trust of the high-profile prisoner Dr Vladimir Krajina. Preucil had tried to elicit information, but Dr Krajina had realised Preucil was on the payroll of the Gestapo.

According to Krajina – in his own evidence to the investigators – Preucil was on good terms with Jockel who gave him cigarettes. (Heinrich Jockel was hanged on 26 October 1946 by the Czech authorities for his management of the concentration camp.) It was because of these actions Krajina claimed his fellow prisoners were suspicious of Augustin Preucil and more cautious in his presence.

Dr Krajina recalled that the other prisoners in close contact with him and Preucil were Karel Hlaváček, a headmaster; Karel Čurda (not the SOE parachutist); Emil Lukes and Josef Tuma, another teacher who died after the liberation in May 1945.

Augustin Preucil told the others in the group that he was a Czech parachutist who had arrived from England, but he later stated he was a pilot who had been shot down over Belgium and captured.

It is clear from Krajina's evidence that the inmates feared one another and there was little trust among them. He told the investigators that they did not trust Emil Lukes as he had given information to Preucil.

Krajina had confided in Lukes, but he revealed to Preucil that a letter from General Ingra, which the professor should have received prior to his arrest and incarceration, was in the possession of someone called Pinca in Prague. Preucil communicated this intelligence in writing to the Gestapo in Prague a few days later.

Krajina claimed to know this, as even the prisoners had their own functioning intelligence network within the prison. The prisoner who told Krajina this, was Robert Hylak (who was later the Secretary of the Union of Liberated Prisoners in Liberec). Soon after Preucil's message, Pinca was arrested by the Gestapo and brought to Terezín before returning to Pankrác Prison in Prague, where he was executed.

Dr Krajina recalled that a Chetnik prison warden named Karel Nejedly, who died in the uprising in May 1945, told him that he had demanded in writing that Preucil be released from custody. To justify this demand, Nejedly stated it was Preucil's information that Pinca was holding the letter from General Ingra that had led to the arrest. Although this was hearsay evidence and could not be verified due to the death of the warden, Dr Krajina believed it to be true. He added that the warden had also said he had seen Preucil's hand-written letter to the Gestapo himself.

This confirmed the Terezín prisoners' suspicions that Preucil was spying on the inmates and sending reports back to the Gestapo. Dr Krajina also mentioned a case which occurred when he was away at Pankrác Prison. Preucil had apparently gained the trust of another prisoner called Holic, by claiming to be a Czech parachutist (Holic was the camp barber). Holic gave

Preucil some news about the progress of the war, which was immediately reported to the Gestapo in Prague. According to Krajina, Holic and a number of other prisoners were taken to a dungeon and tortured, before leaving the camp for an unknown destination. (It has been claimed – see earlier – that Holic was executed.)

In addition, the Chetnik warden Nejedly told Dr Krajina that during these 'interrogations', a girl had told the Gestapo that she had spread war news to the other prisoners, and especially to Preucil.

The Chetnik warden told Dr Krajina that on 31 December 1943, Augustin Preucil, Josef Tuma and Emil Lukes were overheard by a prison guard making fun of Adolf Hitler. As a result, they were all placed in solitary confinement. Augustin Preucil allegedly wrote a letter demanding his release from Terezín, claiming that he had provoked Lukes and Tuma to say such things.

Although a great deal of Dr Krajina's claims, were based on the word of the deceased Chetnik prison warden, it was clear Preucil was heavily involved in provoking and betraying his fellow internees. The question was whether he had been sent to the prison to spy, or was he using his reports and spying in a bid to get released and prove his value and loyalty to the Gestapo?

The fact that Preucil was with Dr Krajina and obtaining intelligence according to the ex-Gestapo man Eska, appears to substantiate the allegation this was a planned term of imprisonment. This is further re-enforced by the assertion of the Gestapo interpreter Josef Chalupský's comment, that

Preucil had looked healthy when he returned from six months in a concentration camp.

Emil Lukes

Emil Lukes told the Czech investigators that he met Preucil in Terezín in 1943, when he was imprisoned for his own political views. Preucil had arrived on 3 November 1943 and immediately told Lukes that he was an English prisoner of war and had escaped from a camp in Berlin. The Gestapo had detained him and sent him to Terezín as he was a Czech airman. (Clearly if all these accounts are true, Preucil was giving various reasons for his detention to different prisoners, men who could easily meet and 'compare notes', exposing Preucil as a spy. It was not good 'trade craft' by the Gestapo agent.)

Lukes said he had trusted Preucil implicitly, especially when he mentioned the names of Czechoslovakian individuals, Lukes knew were in England with the armed forces. He trusted him so much, that he even gave Preucil his warm coat, some food, and other items of clothing.

One day a Gestapo officer called Burian arrived in the prison and spoke with Preucil in front of Lukes. The Gestapo man was unpleasant and eventually he sent Lukes out of the cell. It was clear he wanted to speak with Preucil alone.

The next day, when Preucil was not in the cell, Lukes searched through Preucil's coat pocket and found a Gestapo-issued firearms certificate. Lukes immediately thought Preucil was working for the Gestapo.

Lukes recalled a debate in the cell between himself, Josef Tuma and Preucil. Preucil claimed that the Germans had ordered him to do a radio broadcast and give a report on conditions in England, but he refused to do this. He then claimed he would only make such a report if the Gestapo released him, Tuma and Lukes. Lukes said he protested that Preucil should do such a humiliating thing for their release and said he would not agree to this action.

Emil Lukes told Preucil he had found the firearms certificate in the coat pocket and that he suspected him of being Gestapo. A sharp argument ensued and Lukes berated him for betraying so many Czechoslovakians. Lukes added that over time, he tried to 'win Preucil back to the Czech cause', and it seemed Preucil was showing some signs of remorse.

Over the days following their argument, they debated the same issues a number of times and Preucil even cried at one point. Preucil then told Lukes that he tried to get to Brazil, which was to have been arranged by a man called Karel – a Chief Customs Official from Senflok. He got the papers and went to the Brazilian Consulate, but the Gestapo were waiting and arrested him. The Gestapo said he could work for them or be shot – Preucil had no choice.

Preucil had told Lukes that the Germans took him to the Polish border and allowed him to cross it. He was instructed to join the army (air force) and tasks would be communicated to him via a certain person. After the defeat of Poland, Preucil claimed to have fled with the military through Romania to France, where he fought against the Germans. After France was defeated, he went to England where he became a pilot instructor and married an English woman.

While he was in England, Preucil says he was reproached by the Germans for not working for them. They warned him that if he did not work for Germany, he would be handed over to the English military authorities as a spy. Preucil told Lukes that his new English wife also spied on him. He was afraid he might be brought before the English courts and therefore decided to flee back to the Continent. Preucil told Lukes that at the time he fled, he had been banned from flying; but he was emphatic that he did nothing for the Germans while in England.

Preucil told Lukes that his chance to flee came when he was training two Polish pilots in September 1941. He took off and wanted to detach himself from his charges. During the flight it seemed as though he was being watched, and so he flew out over the sea, but he could not lose the other pilots. In his anger he forgot to turn off his radio receiver which could be used to track him. When he realised, he broke the device and headed into the cloud layer losing the other pilots. He headed south and eventually landed in Belgium. Upon landing he was wounded above the eye and the Germans found him.

Preucil said he was paid 100,000 Koruna for the aircraft and allowed to go home to his parents in Trebsin. He was then forced to work at the Letov aircraft factory and test-fly aircraft. When he refused to do this, Preucil claimed he was arrested and taken to Terezín.

Although this story seemed improbable, Emil Lukes told the investigators he trusted Preucil. He also told them that he could not say whether Preucil spied on other prisoners and supplied information to the Gestapo (despite the evidence of Dr Krajina).

Lukes said he was not 'persecuted' in any way, although he sometimes criticised Preucil for some of his actions. Preucil had never confided in Emil Lukes that he worked for the Gestapo.

There is a clear conflict in the evidence of Dr Krajina and Emil Lukes. Both have their difficulties with validity; Krajina's main source of information was deceased, while Lukes seems to have been keen to over-look some of the words and actions of Preucil, but this may have been to hide his own embarrassment and the fact Pinca had died because of his own loose lips.

Karel Hlaváček

Karel Hlaváček was a headteacher in Vesel near Rovsenko and had lived and worked there since 1929. He told the investigators that he had been arrested on 15 January 1943, by the Gestapo for being anti-German. He was transported initially to the Kartouzy prison, north-east of Prague, before being taken to Pankrác Prison and then on to Terezín concentration camp on 15 May 1943.

In Terezín he was imprisoned with Dr Krajina, Krajina's wife and Josef Tuma, who died of typhus on 20 May 1945. Other prisoners included Karel Čurda and Emil Lukes. As political prisoners they were segregated from the other prisoners and regularly searched by the guards.

On 3 November 1943, 'Gustav' Preucil arrived in their cell. Hlaváček claimed that straight away, the other prisoners suspected he was a Gestapo spy. This was, according to Hlaváček, confirmed when Chetnik Chief Novak warned the political prisoners about Preucil. He told them that on 12 November 1943, the Gestapo at Terezín had been sent a parcel with a message. The wording was not known to Hlaváček, but he said Novak would be able to assist the investigators. (It appears he was never approached and interviewed as there is nothing in the file from this man, he may not have survived.)

As a result of this tip-off, the political prisoners sought to be careful whenever they were in the presence of Augustin 'Gustav' Preucil.

According to Hlaváček, further proof of Preucil's spying for the Gestapo came when he reported the prison barber (Holic) to the Gestapo for spreading news from local factories about the war. He claimed the barber was tortured and placed in solitary confinement. (He did not mention Holic being executed.)

Throughout his time at Terezín, Karel Hlaváček and the others agreed that they would ensure arrangements were made to have Preucil brought to justice after the war.

Hlaváček recalled Augustin Preucil leaving Terezín prison in April or May 1944, but the prisoners did not forget his treachery. Even prison staff, such as Chief Warden Nejedly, were entrusted in ensuring Preucil was dealt with after the war. Unfortunately, as already mentioned, Nejedly was mortally wounded during the post-war coup and died in hospital. It was possibly because of his premature death that Augustin Preucil was not detained as soon as the war ended and the uprising started.

When he was released, Hlaváček said he had taken his own steps to ensure Preucil was dealt with. He sent a message to

Dr Krajina via Air Force Major Tomanek in Prague, warning that Augustin Preucil should be secured as soon as possible.

Karel Hlaváček ended his statement by stating that he had heard from Dr Krajina that Preucil's father had been to his apartment in a bid to make an intervention on behalf of his son. (This is not in any of the case papers relating to Dr Krajina and we cannot confirm this comment, although as we shall see later, he certainly tried to assist his son.)

Chapter Eight

Friends betrayed

Miroslav Hajek

Miroslav Hajek told investigators that he got to know Augustin Preucil in the winter of 1942. Hajek was employed at the School of Art and Design in Prague, as was Max Brantal.

Brantal introduced Hajek to Preucil and they became very good friends, the three men often meeting up for a drink and what Hajek called 'conversations of a most serious kind', some of which were political. Hajek even confided in both men that a relative of his, Karel Ebr, had been arrested and detained by the Gestapo for communist activities.

Hajek stated that their friendship led to trust, and within a couple of weeks of meeting Preucil confided in him that he was an intelligence agent on a 'special mission for the Protectorate of Bohemia and Moravia'. Hajek was, in his own words, 'Struck by Preucil's freedom of movement, the lack of any kind of employment and a particularly positive attitude towards the Germans which was really at odds with his supposed mission as an agent.' It was for this reason that Hajek questioned Max Brantal about Preucil, but he was assured the man was a reliable Czech patriot who Brantal had known during his own military service with the Air Force.

Hajek said his own suspicions were constantly 'exiled by the chivalry' of Preucil, but things changed at the end of November 1944.

The men were in the Metro restaurant in Prague (NB the restaurant was also known as the Vagon and is referred to by both names throughout), when Hajek and Preucil engaged in a heated debate. During the discussion, Preucil cursed the exiled Czechoslovakian President Eduard Benes. Preucil even stated that he hated the president and had never liked him, in fact he would be the first person to remove Benes. The debate descended into a vicious argument and resulted in Hajek calling Preucil a Gestapo agent. Preucil was outraged by this accusation and pulled out a pistol, threatening Hajek with the words, 'You are not the first to go under the turf – I've had a few crises with me anyway.'

Whether anyone intervened and why he was pacified was not mentioned, but Preucil quickly calmed down and put the gun away. The argument seemed to subside and the men parted ways, apparently without any grudges being held. Hajek recalled that the two men met twice more after this incident, but they did not speak.

Hajek told Max Brantal about the argument and the gun in the Metro restaurant. In response, Brantal admitted that he had been thinking things over and he had come to the conclusion that Preucil was a 'lying, cunning and out of character person'. Despite this statement, Hajek claimed Max Brantal continued to meet Preucil and apparently supported him as we have seen in an earlier chapter.

On 13 December 1944, Miroslav Hajek was arrested at the Chetnik station in Reporyje and taken to the Petschek Palace in Prague. He was interrogated by the Gestapo about his behaviour and connections to the communists, before being sent on to Pankrác Prison. A few days later, on 19 December 1944, he was sent to Terezín concentration camp for alleged illegal activities with the communist group in Reporyje, and swearing at the German police. He remained there until the war ended and the uprising in May 1945, when he was transferred to the Na Krete hospital in Terezín suffering from Typhus.

Hajek believed Augustin Preucil was the informant and the cause of his arrest, possibly along with Max Brantal. Later, Hajek was informed by an artist, Stanislav Libensky, that Preucil had a recently completed a portrait of Hajek to send to Hajek's parents. According to the artist, this was because Preucil wanted Hajek's parents to have a reminder of what their son looked like, 'because he would not be going home'. A Mrs Jete Silingeve also allegedly told Hajek that Max Brantal had informed her after the uprising, that Augustin Preucil would destroy Miroslav Hajek at any cost.

Although some of this evidence was hearsay (such as that from Mrs Silingeve and Stanislav Libensky), it was clear that Max Brantal was perhaps very closely aligned to Preucil; who was still making reports to the Gestapo and even betraying his own friends. It is now easy to understand why, for a time, the post-war Czechoslovakian authorities suspected Brantal of collusion with Preucil, and possibly even with the Gestapo.

Bohuslav Cadil

Bohuslav Cadil was another one-time friend of Augustine Preucil. He told the Czech investigators that he got to know Preucil soon after he had moved to Mechenice and drank in the inn owned by Cadil.

Preucil had always behaved and appeared to be very patriotic according to Cadil and he even spread news from London radio (BBC). As a consequence, Cadil freely admitted that he had been listening to the foreign radio stations during the war, and the stories from Preucil corresponded to those he had heard.

Preucil would often speak openly in public against the Nazi regime. In fact, he was so open, Cadil said many villagers thought he must have had Gestapo connections not to fear any repercussions.

In the second half of 1943, Preucil stopped attending Cadil's inn. One day, Preucil's father attended the inn and told Cadil that 'Gustav' had been imprisoned by the Gestapo at the Terezín concentration camp. While Preucil was in the prison, his father would attend the inn once a week and Cadil would give him a double measure of wine.

In spring 1944, Preucil was released from the prison and started to attend Cadil's inn one more. One night, Preucil confided in Cadil that he was, in fact, in the service of the British intelligence services and working against the Germans. He never said anything else or how he came to be in the intelligence services, although he did claim to have joined them before the war had even started.

Cadil said he never spoke in any way to Preucil which might have led to the Gestapo pursuing him. In fact, he even warned Preucil about speaking out-loud in public. Despite this, Preucil once accused Cadil of seeing his gun, a weapon Cadil told the investigators he knew nothing about at that time.

Cadil recalled that during one of their conversations, Preucil had told him he was in France when the war started between France and Germany, working for a Czechoslovakian clothing company called either Rolny or Neher. How he returned to Czechoslovakia from France was never explained, but Preucil did admit to serving in the Czechoslovakian Air Force in peacetime.

Preucil was never seen driving by Cadil, but he often bragged to the inn-keeper and others about his elegant Praga car, which he claimed his father had bought for him in 1938 or 1939.

Around Christmas 1944, Preucil's father attended the inn and told Cadil that his son had to 'hand over a car'. He asked Cadil if he knew any influential people who could intervene in the matter in favour of his son. Cadil could not assist him and the issue of the car was not discussed further, he therefore did not know whether the car was handed over. (Owning and running a car during the occupation was extremely difficult for the average Czechoslovakian, so the investigators were very interested in this point – was it supported by Gestapo funds?)

Cadil told the investigators that in January 1945, he was called in to the Gestapo headquarters in Prague. He was questioned about what he knew of Augustin Preucil, including where he was employed and what he did with his time.

Cadil told the Gestapo that he knew Preucil attended Prague every day for some kind of a job, but he did not know what he did. The Gestapo asked what Preucil talked about and what he said about the German regime. They also asked Cadil about Preucil's parents. Cadil told them that he only knew the parents superficially and that Preucil only spoke about general and indifferent matters. Cadil said he did not mention Preucil giving any information from foreign radio.

Eventually, the Gestapo released Cadil and told him not to tell anyone about his interrogation and their interest in Preucil.

It is clear from this witness and others that the Gestapo were keen to monitor their own agent. After all, they knew he was a former Czech-RAF pilot and that he mixed with all sorts of people around Prague. Anyone who has run or controlled an informant will tell you the individual concerned has to be carefully managed and monitored. This is to ensure they are not misleading you and engaging in their own nefarious activities. The Czech investigators and their associates in the intelligence services would have identified this trend very quickly and assumed the Gestapo were watching 'their man' closely.

About two weeks after Cadil was released by the Gestapo, he saw Preucil at the Mechenice railway station. Preucil immediately accused him of being the reason why the Gestapo was now chasing him. Cadil, naturally wanting a quiet life, told Preucil he had been summoned and interrogated by the Gestapo. They had asked about Preucil's employment, but Cadil assured him he had told them nothing. This seemed to pacify Preucil who went on his way.

A few days later a shoemaker in Mechenice who was an acquaintance of Cadil called Jaroslav Stehlik and told him that Preucil had Gestapo connections, although this was mainly based on the fact, he had an apartment in Prague.

Cadil lost all trust in Preucil and although he still attended the inn and spoke with him, Cadil was careful not to say anything that might be used against him.

As the Russian army moved towards Budapest in early 1945, the London (BBC) radio stated that the Nazis had shot a number of Russian parliamentarians. A few days later, the German radio commented on this news, denying such reports. By pure chance, Preucil was present in the inn and asked Cadil what was new. Mistakenly, Cadil told him what the foreign radio station had said about the Budapest incident.

Ten to fourteen days later, on 24 February 1945, Chetnik officers arrested Cadil and took him to the Gestapo office in Benešov. After interrogation, Cadil was told he was being charged with listening to foreign radio broadcasts, which he strenuously denied.

While in custody, Cadil says he became aware that Professor Josef Hurt had also been arrested and detained at Benešov for similar reasons. The Gestapo showed Cadil a statement written by Josef Hurt, in which the professor admitted listening to the Beremunser radio station with him. As a consequence, with little room to manoeuvre, Cadil confessed to knowing Hurt and listening to the radio station.

Cadil told the Czech investigators that he had requested a confrontation with his accuser in Benešov, but this was denied. The Gestapo Kommissar told him, in German, that he should not wish for a confrontation, as he was being accused by a Gestapo agent. If the source of the information was identified, Cadil 'could never be released'.

Cadil wisely did not pursue this request, but believed Preucil to have been the informant. During the interrogation by the Gestapo, Cadil had seen their file on the desk, it contained a document signed in the name of Josef Sifrou.

Cadil was taken to the Terezín concentration camp and remained there until liberation on the 7 May 1945. He was lucky to have only been incarcerated for less than three months and to survive.

While incarcerated in Terezín, Cadil said he had spoken with a man called Ladislav Skvor. He told Cadil that he had read reports filed against him by the Gestapo in Benešov and these were signed by Augustin Preucil. Skvor said he had been detained for running away from work and attempting to forge documents.

Cadil told the investigators that he knew Preucil had maintained some love affairs with what he called 'wild women'. One such woman was called Ella. She was described by Cadil as being 25 years old, with striking big eyes and bleached hair. He also believed Preucil saw another woman from Hvozdnice to the south of Prague (believed to be Jirina Vanisova).

It was clear from the evidence of both Cadil and Hajek, that Preucil was happy to befriend people and obtain information which he provided to the Gestapo – almost certainly for financial reward. However, while the men were mistreated in prison and Hajek contracted typhus, the third prisoner mentioned in this section – Professor Josef Hurt (sometimes spelt as Hurta) was less fortunate. In the court case papers there is a simple memorandum it is titled: 'Professor Josef Hurt (death notice).' It states: 'The liquidation group of the former German prison/Gestapo/Terezín, Small Fortress announces that Mr Josef Hurt born April 11th 1881, died on April 15, 1945 at 6pm in cell C.41 and was buried at the Small Fortress. Please accept our deepest condolences.'

The notice had apparently been sent to his relatives to inform them of his death. Hurt had studied at the Academy of Arts, Architecture and Design in Prague. Later in life he worked as an artist and was a renowned theatre director, but by 1945, when denounced by Preucil, he was a frail old man. He was too weak to survive Terezín.

Maria Dostalova

Maria Dostalova gave evidence to the investigation team, stating that she was a close friend of Professor Josef Hurt.

She knew that Hurt had told Augustin Preucil he had been listening to foreign radio stations, as Hurt told her this himself.

Preucil had presented himself to her and others as a Czech Air Force pilot who had flown with the English. He was always very patriotic and praised his home nation.

On one occasion, Hurt told Maria that Preucil had warned him that the inn-keeper, Bohuslav Cadil, was in the service of the Gestapo and he should be careful in his presence.

She recalled Josef Hurt being arrested by the Chetniks in early 1945, and being taken to the Gestapo in Benešov. They held him there until 27 March, when he was transferred to

Terezín prison. Maria said she had managed to visit him once while in custody at Benešov and he told her he was detained for listening to foreign radio stations. However, he did not say who had reported him to the authorities. As we know, Hurt died in Terezín on 15 April 1945, just before the end of the war – too frail to stand the rigours of the camp.

Maria Dostalova told the Czech investigators that she suspected Preucil of being the informant and in August 1945, she went to Benešov where Gestapo Kommissioner Hugo Heller was held in custody. He had dealt with both Hurt and Cadil when they were arrested and she managed to speak to him. There was a heated argument between them concerning the arrest and treatment of the two men, but eventually Heller calmed down and told her that there was a Gestapo agent in Mechenice involved in their arrests. When she asked him directly whether that agent was Augustin Preucil, he answered with all certainty – 'Yes'.

The investigators could now see that the accounts of the prisoners and even Hugo Heller of the Gestapo, corroborated one another. Not only had Augustin Preucil fled with the Hurricane and betrayed the Belgian civilians, but he was betraying the Czech people – including people who were his friends. Why he would do such a thing to his own friends is incomprehensible.

Josef Vitejcek

Josef Vitejcek ran a small barber's shop in Mechenice. He had run the business since September 1938 and was a well-known figure in the town.

Vitejcek told the Czech investigators that Augustin Preucil started to attend his business as a customer in 1942. Initially, he was just a customer, but they soon became good friends and he trusted the young man.

Eventually, Preucil told Vitejcek that he was in the service of the English intelligence service and working against the German authorities. He had been in England, but how he had returned to Czechoslovakia was never disclosed by Preucil.

Vitejcek knew that Preucil was imprisoned in Terezín because his father had told him this (just like he had told the inn-keeper Cadil). When Augustin was released, Vitejcek told him that conditions there must be terrible for the Jews, as he had heard this on the English radio broadcasts and 3,000 people had died in the prison.

In May 1944, not long after Preucil's release, Vitejcek said he told Preucil that he listened to the foreign radio station at a friend's home and while tuning the radio, they had picked up a French station.

On 2 September 1944, Vitejcek was arrested by the Benešov Gestapo and accused of listening to a foreign radio station at a friend's house in May 1944. He was also accused of spreading reports of Jewish deaths in Terezín prison and making offensive comments about Adolf Hitler.

Vitejcek denied the allegations, but under torture he says he finally confessed to listening to the London radio and once listening to another foreign radio station. He continued to deny making any comments about Hitler, but after further torture during which he was struck with fists and a length of rope, he also admitted to this.

The information in the Gestapo files was handwritten and he could not make out what it actually said, but a Gestapo interpreter told him that he must have an acquaintance who tipped them off. The only person Vitejcek knew he had ever told about the Jews in Terezín, the foreign radio and the friend's house was Augustin Preucil.

Vitejcek was taken before the German court in Tabor and taken to Pankrác Prison in Prague. On 4 November 1944, he was sentenced to two years imprisonment and taken to the penitentiary at Bernau. He was then moved on to Golnov and on 5 March 1945, he was moved to Freiberg, sub-camp of Flossenburg concentration camp near Rostock in Germany. He was liberated by the Red Army on 3 May 1945 and made his own way home to Czechoslovakia.

The investigators decided to confront Augustin Preucil with Josef Vitejcek in Pankrác Prison. When the two men met, Vitejcek told Preucil:

> I spoke exclusively to you about the fact that I was listening to a foreign radio station at my friend Solce's and that London radio announced that 3,000 Jews had perished in Terezín at the hands of the Germans. At the Gestapo in Benešov, these comments were repeated and I was therefore convicted. Only you could have tipped them off.

Preucil replied:

> I don't remember talking to the witness about listening to the radio, I didn't give it.

Vitejcek continued:

> I had a conversation about listening to a foreign radio station with you in May 1944, at night on the road in the Douce near the fire station in Mechenice.

Preucil replied:

> I don't remember that conversation. I definitely did not give the Gestapo anything.

The net was closing on Preucil, but still he kept up his various excuses.

The Czech investigators continued with their efforts and soon located Ladislav Skvor, the man mentioned by Bohuslav Cadil.

Ladislav Skvor

Ladislav Skvor told the investigators that he lived in Mechenice and knew Preucil after he had arrived from Trebsin in 1942. The two men became good friends and would watch football together, often meeting in a restaurant near his friend Bohuslav Cadil's inn in the town.

Skvor told his interviewers that he was young and did not care much about politics and so he never discussed such subjects with Augustin Preucil.

Preucil was always apparently very patriotic and warned Skvor that the inn-keeper Bohuslav Cadil was actually a

Above: left to right B. Kymlicka, J. Kucera, R. Zima, Preucil, J. Pardus, B. Postrekovsky, T. Vybiral, F. Sticka, A. Vrana, M. Standera and M. Kopecky at Chartres, France early 1940. *Below*: Chartres 25 Jan 1940, Preucil is on the left of the front two men. (Images courtesy of Tom Dolezal, B & E Kudlacek collection Free Czech AF Association)

Left: Czech air force image of Preucil. (Courtesy -Josef 'Joe' Vochyán / cestiarafaci website)

Below: Augustin Preucil in 1946-47. (Dept. of Documentation & History, Czech Prison Service)

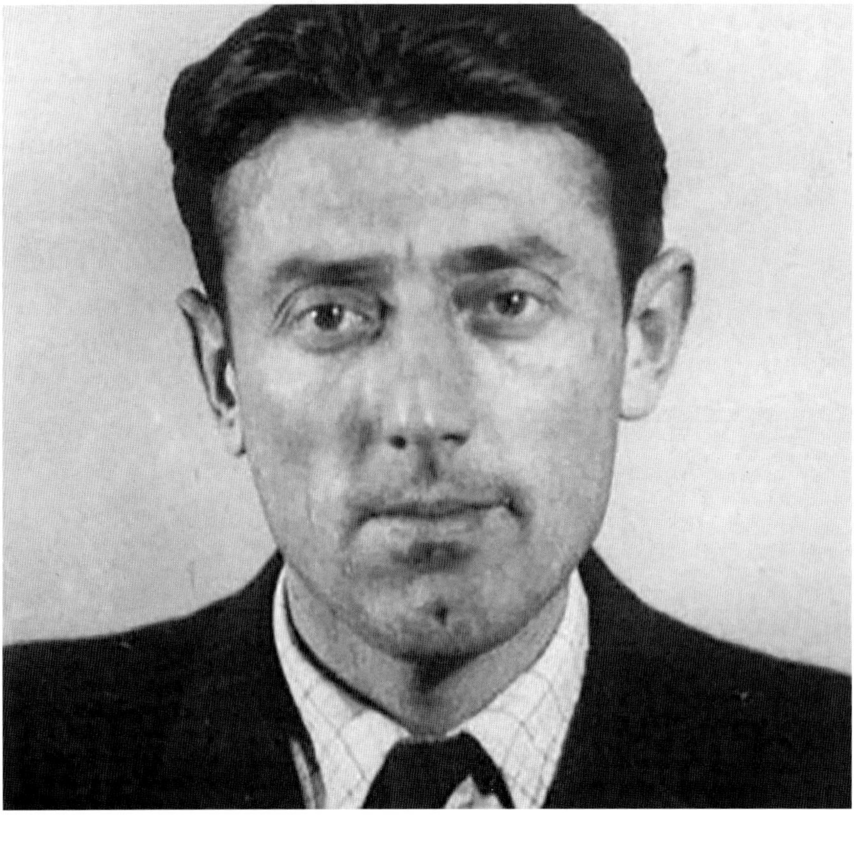

A 1942 RAF aerial view of Usworth, with Sunderland, the River Wear and the North Sea in the background. Murial lived top right of the image. (Imperial War Museum)

Above: An image from about 1942 of Preucil's 'stolen' 55 OTU Hurricane in the museum in Berlin before it was destroyed in an allied air raid in 1943. (German National Aviation Museum via Richard Chapman c/o Aeroplane Magazine 2003)

Below: 55 OUT at RAF Usworth, 17th June 1941. Preucil is on the rear row, third from the right. (Image courtesy of Tom Dolezal, B & E Kudlacek collection Free Czech AF Association)

Oskar Fleischer who recruited Augustin Preucil. A criminal Inspector in Department III A (Counter Intelligence & Treason) of the Prague Gestapo & below: Karel Curda. (Both in public domain, copyright unknown and untraceable)

```
Reichssicherheitshauptamt                                    57
       Nachrichten-Uebermittlung

13³⁰  2 DEZ 1941

Geheime Reichssache

H.-O. Nr. _____   Telegramm — Funkspruch — Fernschreiben
                              Fernspruch

+ BERLIN NUE 195 119 2/12/41 1325 -MA- =
AN H-STUF. RUTZEN, PRAG/ BURG ==
G E H E I M E   R E I C H S S A C H E ==
VORG.: DORTG. G.RS. NR. 25/41 ==
BETR.: RUECKKEHR DES V-MANNES AUGUSTIN
P R E U C I L. ==
DER GESAMTVORGANG IST DER LESEMAPPE DES
OBERGRUPPENFUEHRERS BEIGEFUEGT. -
ANFRAGE: SIND DIE WEISUNGEN DES OBERGRUPPENFUEHRERS
1.) 5.000,- RM BELOHNUNG (FUENFTAUSEND) -
2.) BRIEF AN H-GRUF. MUELLER UND AN DAS OKW AMT
AUSLANDSABWEHR Z.HD. OBERS BENTIVEGNIS -
3.) UNTERRICHTUNG VON REICHSMARSCHALL ,
REICHSFUEHRER-H, REICHSAUSSENMINISTER, H-GRUF. SCHAUB
UND GENERAL BODENSCHATZ - DER STAATSPOLIZEILEITSTELLE
PRAG WEITERGEGEBEN ?? ==

     DER CHEF DER SIPO UND DES SD - AJUTANT -
     BNR. 54661/41 G.RS. - (GEZ.: WERTH) +
```

Gestapo / SS message cover dated 2nd December 1941 noting the 'return' of Preucil and the reward of 5,000 Reichsmarks. The English translation is on the next page. (State Regional Archive in Prague, Extraordinary People's Court Prague, sign. Ls 9/46)

REICH SECURITY MAIN OFFICE

Messaging

13:30   2 Dec. 1941

SECRET MATTER

Berlin now 195 119 2/12/41 at 13:35

To SS Stauf Rutzen Prague / Burg

Return of airman Augustin PREUCIL.

The entire process is attached to the folder of the upper group leader.

Requested are the instructions of the Ober Gruppen fuehrer:

1. 5000 Reich marks reward (Five thousand)
2. A letter to SS Gruppen Fuhrer Meuller and the OKW AMT foreign defence Z.HD. Oberst Bentivegnis.
3. Information from Reichs Marshal, Reichs Fuhrer SS, Reich Foreign Minister SS Gruppen Fuhrer Schaub and General Bodenschatz – passed on to the Prague State Police Headquarters.

The head of the Sipo and SD adjutant BNR.

....

Author's notes to the above:

Gruppen Fuhrer Julius Schaub???? Adjutant and assistant to Hitler, Reichs Fuhrer SS was Himmler

General Karl Bodenschatz liaison between Hitler and Goring – the head of the Luftwaffe.

It is interesting to note this only says 5,000 Reichsmarks not 10,000 RM.

The Russlova Street Church in Prague where the SOE agents who assassinated Heydrich were corned and killed in a gun battle with SS troops. (Author)

Right: The air vent to the crypt is still surrounded by German bullet holes. (Authors image)

Below: An old image of Gerik & Curda on trial in the Extraordinary Peoples Court in Prague, April 1947. Gerik is on the left and Curda on the right. (Copyright unknown and untraceable- widely in public domain)

Above left and above right: Major Jan Ambrus & Alexander Hesse, both men were with Preucil at Chartres. (All images courtesy of Josef 'Joe' Vochyán the cestiarafaci website)

Below left and below right: Sergeant Vaclav Brejcha served with Preucil on 43 Sqn and was mentioned in his evidence to investigators & Major/FTL: Stanislav Rejthar who gave evidence.

FTL's Frantisek Burda (top) & Ivo Tonder were confronted by Preucil while in Gestapo custody in 1944. (Courtesy of Josef 'Joe' Vochyán the cestiarafaci website)

GELÖBNIS

GEMÄSS § 2, ABS. 1 DES DEKRETS DES STAATSPRÄSIDENTEN VOM 8. MÄRZ 1940, SLG. No 83.

Ich gelobe, dem Führer des Grossdeutschen Reiches, Adolf Hitler, als dem Schutzherrn des Protektorates Böhmen und Mähren Gehorsam zu leisten, die Belange des Grossdeutschen Reiches zum Wohle des Protektorates Böhmen und Mähren zu fördern, die Anordnungen des Oberhauptes und der Regierung des Protektorates Böhmen und Mähren zu befolgen, die Gesetze zu beachten und meine Amtspflichten gewissenhaft zu erfüllen.

_____, den 23. VI. 1944

Preucil Augustin
(eigenhändige Unterschrift)

Parle-Michenice 130
(Wohnort)

Preucil's signed attestation to be loyal to Adolf Hitler and the Reich dated the 23rd June 1944. (State Regional Archive in Prague, Extraordinary People's Court Prague, sign. Ls 9/46)

PERSONALBEHÖRDE:	Versorgungsamt I Prag	Anlage B.
(Anstalt, Unternehmung, Fonds)	Prag VII., Messepalast	
OSOBNÍ ÚŘAD:		Formblatt 2.
(Ústav, podnik, fond)		Vzorec 2.

Anzeige über Verheiratung.
Oznámení o sňatku.

Am .... habe/beabsichtige ich mit der/dem ....
Dne **2. 7. 1941** uzavřel(a) jsem sňatek / ~~zamýšlím uzavříti sňatek~~ s ....

geborenen / rozenou **Kirby Muriel**   religiöses Bekenntnis / náboženského vyznání **protestant**

geboren in / narozenou-ým v **Sunderland** am / dne **22. 4. 1922**

die Ehe geschlossen. / zu schließen.

Ich versichere auf Ehre und Gewissen, daß ich die umseitig angeführten Angaben nach bestem Wissen gemacht habe und daß mir keine Umstände bekannt sind, die die Annahme rechtfertigen könnten, daß meine — zukünftige — Ehefrau — Ehemann*) von jüdischen Eltern oder Großeltern abstammt. Ich weiß, daß wissentlich falsche Angaben nach den einschlägigen Dienststrafvorschriften geahndet werden und daß ich, wenn sich die Angaben über die nichtjüdische Abstammung als unrichtig herausstellen, jedenfalls die fristlose Entlassung aus dem Dienst (§ 7 der RegVO Slg. Nr. 137/1942) zu gewärtigen habe.

Ujišťuji na svou čest a svědomí, že údaje uvedené na rubu jsem učinil podle svého nejlepšího vědomí a že mi nejsou známy žádné okolnosti, které by mohly odůvodniti domněnku, že moje — můj — budoucí manželka — manžel*) pocházejí od židovských rodičů nebo prarodičů. Vím, že vědomě nesprávné údaje se stíhají podle příslušných disciplinárních předpisů a že, ukáží-li se údaje o nežidovském původu nesprávnými, musím v každém případě počítati s okamžitým propuštěním ze služby (§ 7 vl. nař. Sb. č. 137/1942).

V **Prag** den **23 VI.** 194 **4**

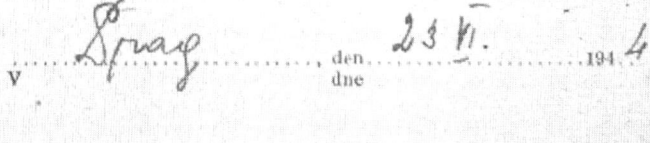

Preucil's signed declaration also dated 23rd June 1944 stating that he was married to Muriel Kirby, born in Sunderland on the 22nd April, 1922. (State Regional Archive in Prague, Extraordinary People's Court Prague, sign. Ls 9/46)

The 'Cinema room' in Gestapo HQ in Pecks Palace, Prague. Arriving prisoners would be made to sit on the benches and look at the far wall while guards with batons paraded up and down, striking anyone who did not comply. This is probably the location Preucil met the others. (Author)

A cell in the basement of the Gestapo HQ in Prague. These small unlit units were once safety deposit rooms in the Jewish bank that occupied the building before the arrival of the Gestapo. It was in cells like these that the prisoners who witnessed Preucil were located. (Author)

German-Czechoslovakian agent Karl Richter who may or may not have been involved with Preucil in England. (UK National Archives Contains public sector information licensed under the Open Government Licence V3)

Gestapo agent. Later Skvor discovered it was the other way around and Cadil was innocent of such charges.

Skvor also knew the barber, Josef Vitejcek, and did talk with him about politics before he was arrested, (this being contrary to earlier declaration of having no interest in such matters). In addition, he knew Josef Hurt, who he described as an artist and theatre director who was also detained and subsequently died in Terezín concentration camp. Skvor knew that Hurt had been to Cadil's inn and restaurant which Preucil frequented.

In February 1944, Skvor was forced to go and work in Aschaffenburg in Germany. He did not like this and three months later, in May 1944, he returned to Mechenice without permission. Once he was home, he would often meet with Preucil who knew he had run away from work in Germany.

One day, Preucil asked Skvor if he was afraid the authorities would prosecute him for running away from his work in Germany. Skvor clearly was concerned, but Preucil advised that he should get some sort of a report which would state he was actually employed in Prague. Preucil then offered to type up such a report himself, because he had a typewriter at his disposal in his office in Prague. However, Preucil pointed-out that he did not have an official stamp to validate the report and therefore Skvor would have to obtain a fake stamp himself.

Skvor told the Czech interviewers that no one else was present when he had this conversation with Preucil, it had taken place on a roadside in Mechenice and the area was completely deserted. Skvor was at pains to say he did not even tell his own parents or relatives about this fake report.

Augustin Preucil never obtained the false report for him, but about three weeks after their meeting on 27 October 1944, Skvor was detained by Chetnik's from Davli and taken to the Gestapo office in Benešov. The Chetniks knew Skvor had run away from work in Germany, but they never reported this. In fact, en route to Benešov the escorting Chetnik sergeant told Skvor that he did not know why he was escorting him to the Gestapo.

The Gestapo in Benešov accused Skvor of trying to obtain a false employment confirmation report and asked him where he hid the false stamp. Skvor denied everything, but the Gestapo Kommissar dealing with the case wanted to know where he got the confirmation report from.

Skvor did not mention Preucil to the Gestapo man and continued to deny everything. The Gestapo official told him he did not believe him and that his denials were in vain, as he was already aware of the full facts. The Gestapo man then showed Skvor a report which stated the detainee had in his possession a confirmation of work document and that he needed a fake stamp to validate it.

The document he was shown was machine signed with the name 'Augustin Preucil' on it. The report, Skvor told the investigators, contained the sentence, 'My friend has a confirmation of employment and a stamp at home'. The report was written in Czech not German and Skvor said he was interrogated in Czech not German by Kommissar Riha.

As a result of this information and his interrogation, Skvor was taken to the prison at Terezín. He was detained there for five and a half months before being transferred to the concentration camp at Flossenberg in Bavaria. Skvor was eventually released by the advancing Allies, but he was so ill and weak that he had to be admitted to the hospital in Cham.

Like Vitejcek, Skvor was confronted with Augustin Preucil by the Czech investigators. Preucil stated:

> The witness knows I never talked to him about any confirmation of employment, nor did I ever give it. On the contrary, I had the impression that he was guarding me on the orders of the Gestapo.

Skvor replied,

> I insist on the content of my testimony in full. I spoke only and exclusively to the accused about the confirmation in question.

The investigators now knew that as well as liaising and assisting traitors like Karel Čurda, Viliam Gerik, Grabovsky and Kindl, Preucil had betrayed innocent patriots like Cadil, Hajek, Hurt, Skvor and Vitejcek. This was in addition to working as a Gestapo agent in the air force and stealing the Hurricane fighter in 1941.

It appeared that this man, who did not have an apparent occupation – despite the regime forcing people to work – was working for the Gestapo and effectively selling his friends and associates for reward money.

However, more revelations were to follow with allegations being made by a wide range of people including girlfriends and captured Czechoslovakian airmen.

Chapter Nine

Milena and Karel Tomanova

One incident that Augustin Preucil was happy to admit – or at least partly admit – to was that concerning the Tomanova family and the rogue Special Operations Executive parachutist Viliam Gerik. The Czech investigators were consequently quick to locate and interview those named by Preucil, enabling them to unpick his story.

Milena Tomanova

Milena Tomanova explained to the investigators that she had lived at 31, Dejvicka, Prague, XIX since 1932, and worked as a sales assistant in the city. She had one sister called Jarmila who was by 1945 married, but before the war she was in a relationship with a man called Vaclav Modrak. Modrak had apparently fled the country when the Germans took control and he went to England with the Free Czech forces. Since that time, the family had heard nothing from him apart from an approach by a stranger in 1942.

In March or April 1942, Milena said her father Karel told her that a young Czechoslovakian man had been into his shop and claimed to be a parachutist from England. The man begged her father for help as he was stranded and wanted to give him money for food and assistance. Her father said he would not accept the money, but he gave the young man some food vouchers so he could at least get himself something to eat. The young man told Milena's father that he would have to turn himself in to the Gestapo, as there was no way out and he had no other option but to surrender himself.

In August 1942, the same young man who Milena recognised from her father's previous description, came to the family apartment in Prague. Milena said she immediately assumed he must have given himself up to the Gestapo and been interrogated before being released. The man told her he had surrendered to the Gestapo and was now working for them – but in reality, he was working against them.

The young man then said he knew Sergeant Valcav Modrak who was in England, and he was to pass on greetings from him to the Tomanova family. Milena said they talked for a while and the man gave his name as Viliam Gerik before he left the apartment.

In November 1942, she claimed that Viliam Gerik attended her father's shop once again. This time he showed her father a Gestapo identification card with his name on it.

Milena told the investigators that she was at that time, getting concerned about the man who was clearly working for the Gestapo. Frightened, she contacted an old friend called Max Brantal. After telling Brantal what had happened, he told her he had a friend called Augustin Preucil, who had also arrived as a parachutist from England and was completely reliable, he would know what to do.

Brantal introduced Milena to Preucil in the street, and she told him what had happened with Viliam Gerik. Immediately,

Preucil warned her about Gerik, saying he worked for the Gestapo and that, along with another man called Jerhod (Karel Čurda), they had betrayed the parachutists in the Resslova Street church following the assassination of Heydrich. Preucil told her that both men had been rewarded by the Gestapo and could not be trusted as they were traitors.

Milena admitted to the investigators that she wanted to get rid of Gerik, so she told Preucil he had invited her father to go to Brno. Gerik, she explained, wanted her father to take part in some form of action against the Germans. However, she then explained to the investigators that this was completely untrue, but she told Preucil this to get rid of Gerik and protect her family.

Milena continued her evidence stating that a day or so later, Preucil attended her home with a man called 'Chalupovsky' (this was clearly Josef Chalupský). The two men showed her a series of photographs of men in uniform and civilian clothes, asking if she could identify the man Gerik among the images. However, Milena claimed she could not identify Viliam Gerik from the images. Preucil again told Milena that he knew Gerik well and he was not to be trusted.

Shortly afterwards, Milena was summoned to the Gestapo headquarters and questioned about Viliam Gerik. She told the Czech investigators that she had admitted to the Gestapo, that he had attended their home several times and Gerik said he was a parachutist from England. She also told the Gestapo she had not reported Gerik to the Gestapo as he initially said he was going to surrender himself and later showed her his Gestapo identification card. This seemed to satisfy the Gestapo officers who directed her to notify them immediately, if he ever attended their home or shop again.

Viliam Gerik never attended their address again, but in March 1943, Milena was once again summoned to the Gestapo headquarters in Prague. This time her father was also summoned.

At the Petschek Palace they were met by Gestapo Kommissar Sulc, who confronted them with Viliam Gerik. (I have been unable to identify Sulc.) What was said in the confrontation was not recorded in the court file for Preucil. Milena was interrogated about her contacts with Gerik, but she stood by her original statement.

Milena and her father were eventually released by the Gestapo, but in the hallway of the building, she was asked what work hours her father undertook and whether they were long or short. Later, when she spoke to her father, she found that Gerik had claimed her father worked long hours.

As the Tomanovs left the Gestapo headquarters they were told by an escorting official that the 'Sword of Damocles' had been hanging over them both since November. Milena claimed she did not know what this meant, but thought it meant the Gestapo had been watching them.

Milena admitted to the Czech interviewers that she was getting very close to Preucil at that time. He bought her a ring, a fine coat, a small dog and a bag full of Christmas presents. She told Preucil about the summons to the Gestapo headquarters and he promised to find out from Josef Chalupský what was going on with Gerik.

Preucil soon told Milena that Viliam Gerik had been arrested and imprisoned – or even executed – by the Gestapo. However, a short time later, Preucil told her that he had seen Gerik free and at large in Prague. He also believed the interrogation of Tomanovs was just a distraction and staged by the Gestapo to cover Gerik.

Milena told the investigators that Preucil had never admitted to her that he was in the employment of the Gestapo. He told her he only knew the Czech Gestapo interpreter Chalupský, who worked for the Gestapo and would occasionally give him information.

Milena said she liked Preucil and thought he had loved her. Despite Max Brantal having initially told her Preucil was a parachutist, she told the investigators that he told her himself, he had fled from England as he thought they had something against him. He landed in Belgium and the Germans arrested him. Preucil claimed the Germans let him go free as they couldn't do anything with him. However, on another occasion, Preucil had told Milena that he had flown from England during an air show in front of the exiled Czech President Eduard Benes and landed in France. He said he could never tell her the truth and would explain everything once the war was over.

Preucil had money and didn't hide this fact from Milena, claiming to have received the money as a parachutist via the Czech resistance.

Milena told them that in June 1943, the couple broke off their relationship as she did not like him anymore, but she did not know he worked for the Gestapo. Preucil only ever claimed to be working against the Germans and that was his assignment from

England, but she had noticed contradictions in his accounts. However, even when she noticed these contradictions, she assumed he could not tell the truth for military reasons and she did not challenge him.

Milena said she had continued to see Preucil in the street and spoke with him occasionally, but that in 1944, Max Brantal told her he was in Terezín prison. He was later released and worked in Prague, but she could not state anything more about him after that time.

Karel Tomanova

Karel Tomanova told the investigators that he had two daughters, Milena and Jarmila.

In March 1942, a young man came to him and showed him a police issue social security card from Brno. He said he was a parachutist and had dropped from an English plane in Moravia. He told Karel that he had been given his address by Sergeant Modrak, Jarmila's fiancé and that he brought greetings from him in England.

The man wanted to give Karel money and said he was hungry, but Karel gave him some bread and meat while declining his money. The man said he could not get any help anywhere and was going to register with the local police office. This made Karel cautious and suspicious, but after a while the young man left. Karel immediately informed his family, including Milena, about the man and what was said.

Karel told the investigators that in about October 1942, the same man came to him and said he had registered with the Gestapo. He claimed this action had saved his life and he produced a Gestapo identification card in the name of Viliam Gerik. Karel was unsure with his recollections, but he told the Czech investigators that it was possible Gerik had also admitted to working for the Czechoslovakian resistance at this time.

Karel said he did not trust Gerik and when he told his wife and Milena about this man, they too said he had visited the family home, showed them his ID card and claimed that he was working for the Czech cause.

The investigators asked Karel about whether Gerik had ever invited him to Brno for a meeting (as related by Milena). He said he had never been invited to any such meeting by Gerik, meaning that Milena's assertion this was fabricated to rid the family of Gerik was indeed true.

Karel said he was summoned in March 1943 to the Petschek Palace, where the Gestapo asked him about Gerik, but he claimed he did not know him. Gerik was suddenly brought into the room and confronted with Karel. Gerik said he had been to his property to bring greetings from Modrak in England and he had wanted to entrust Karel with some money. Karel had given him food stamps. The Gestapo then asked Karel what clothing he wore in the shop. When Karel described his usual attire at work, Gerik had claimed the clothing was different, before he was removed and taken away by the Gestapo guards.

Karel said he assumed Gerik had been arrested at this point, as he noticed he had no laces in his shoes. Eventually, having also summoned his daughter Milena and questioned her about Gerik and his work clothing, the Tomanovs were released by the Gestapo. On the way out, Karel recalled being warned that the 'Sword of Damocles' was hanging over both Milena and himself.

In April 1943, Karel met Preucil while out walking. He had seen him once before with his daughter Milena at a concert in the town hall. He said Preucil was very friendly with Milena at that time and bought her some gifts. Preucil told Karel that he should not trust Gerik, he was the 'Greatest murderer and was responsible for all of Lidice.' (The small town of Lidice was destroyed and most of the population murdered by the SS/Gestapo in revenge for the assassination of Heydrich. Those children not murdered and deemed Germanic, were sent to Germany.)

Karel told the investigators that Preucil was very relaxed and told him he could be trusted, as he was a Czechoslovakian agent himself. Karel Tomanova was keen to point out that he had always wanted Milena to renounce her acquaintance with Preucil, and she eventually did so in the summer of 1943.

He was concerned he may be arrested by the Gestapo straight after the first visit of Gerik, but this did not occur. He told Milena this and she said he should not worry about Gerik, as it was his own concern. Karel said he did not know anything else and to the day of his interview with the Czech investigators, Milena had not told him whether she was directly involved in Gerik's arrest by the Gestapo.

It was clear that Milena did not tell her father everything about Viliam Gerik or Augustin Preucil. She seems to have been a cautious woman, but she could also be liberal with the truth and clearly fabricated an allegation to the Gestapo to rid the family of Gerik. The question is why did she say this? Was she so worried about Gerik and her family, or had she been coerced by Preucil and asked or directed to say this?

Sergeant Modrak does not appear to have been traced and interviewed by the Czech investigation team. Did he survive the war? I have been unable to positively identify this man, but he seems to have existed.

The Gestapo were quick to react and on the 6 April 1943, Viliam Gerik was arrested and sent to Pankrác Prison in Prague. He was soon moved on to Terezín concentration camp and then to Dachau concentration camp, before being liberated and returning to Prague in May 1945.

Viliam Gerik did not try to hide himself when he returned to his homeland, clearly feeling he was an innocent Czech patriot. He was soon arrested and sent to Pankrác Prison.

In recent years, there has been a ground swell of public opinion in the Czech Republic, with many people feeling that Gerik was a victim of circumstance who found himself in an invidious position in 1942. Later he was betrayed by Preucil, but he was one of the three names on the Czechoslovakian authorities most wanted list in 1945.

Chapter Ten

Others linked to Preucil

As the investigators continued to trawl through the Gestapo records and interview those connected to Augustin Preucil, they found his lies and treachery went deeper and deeper.

It was clear that Preucil would often state that he was either a parachutist, or in the service of the British secret service, but on occasion he would also claim to be a shot down and an escaped prisoner of war. He would try to deflect any suspicions by telling his associates that he could not tell them everything and would do so after the war's conclusion. This may seem illogical in 2023, but in a nation under Nazi occupation where no one could be trusted and thousands had been executed, it was better to keep your mouth shut and remain silent. For this reason, many people chose, like the Police Station Commander Ludvík Němec in Trebsin, to keep quiet.

When interrogated, Preucil had claimed that he assisted people like General Vaclav Engler, who he was supposed to have spied upon for the Gestapo.

General Vaclav Engler

Engler was interviewed by the investigation team and stated that since 1941, he had been employed in the Supply Office at the Veletrzny Palace in Prague. He told them that he was made head of the department and the group. (After the occupation by the Nazis, many officials and military personnel were employed in public services. The new regime needed to ensure the state system functioned efficiently and these individuals were also easily traceable if the Gestapo wanted to spy on them.)

In 1943, the Secretary to the Head of the Welfare Office (Lieutenant Adamek), alerted Engler to the fact that a certain Augustin Preucil, who had been assigned to the office, seemed to be a Gestapo agent. Adamek had apparently learned this from his German superior, although no name was given.

In time, Preucil approached Engler and told him that he was deployed by the Gestapo to the Supply Office to guard him and the other colonels employed there. Preucil had also disclosed that he knew General Kratochvila was worried about eavesdropping of conversations by the Gestapo – a clear indication that this newcomer knew what was going on throughout the building.

It appears that by this time, Preucil was starting to worry about what would happen to him after the war. Engler said Preucil begged him to testify in his favour, once the Czech government was restored. He told Engler he was loyal patriot who had served in England with a fighter squadron and with Major Hess of the Czechoslovakian Air Force.

He wanted Engler to confirm that he had been open and honest about his supposed work for the Gestapo, and that he had sought to assist the loyal Czechs in the building. Engler told the investigators, that he had shared the comments of Preucil with Colonel Taskovi, who was in charge of the office, and he could confirm these facts.

Engler concluded by telling the investigators that he didn't speak with Preucil again until the start of May 1945, as the war ended. It was obvious to Engler that Preucil was clearly afraid and he begged the general to protect his parents from the hatred of the local population. Preucil was also fearful that the Germans would shoot him at the last moment. Finally, Preucil asked the general to remember the two traitors Čurda and Gerik, who betrayed the parachutists at the church after the Heydrich affair.

We see here once again, the tactic of Preucil in asking the individual to remember that he had helped them, and that they should ensure Gerik and Čurda were punished after the liberation.

Augustin Preucil was a manipulator and a liar who sowed confusion, but his actions were starting to catch up with him. He had claimed in his own interrogation that, with the help of his cousin (Augustin Povolny), he had warned another man called Kopecke that he was being watched by the Gestapo.

Augustin (or Gustav) Povolvy

The investigators located Augustin Povolvy and interviewed him. He said he knew Preucil and that he was a pilot in England before returning home to his village at Trebsin. After this, Preucil had moved to Mechenice, but the two of them were not in regular contact. There was no confirmation in his statement and evidence that he was actually Preucil's cousin.

Povolvy knew that Preucil had been imprisoned in Terezín concentration camp and after his release, he worked at the

Office of Supply in the Veletrzny Palace in Prague. At the time, Povolvy said he worked as a janitor in the Trznica restaurant in Rytirska Street in Prague.

One day Povolvy was at work and Preucil came into the restaurant. He directed Povolvy to call a man from the public telephone booth. He was given a telephone number and told to call a switchboard, which would connect him to the line he requested (provided by Preucil). He would speak to a man and on the directions of Preucil, tell him to, 'Be careful and take care of himself', before hanging up. Povolvy was not to give the man his name and Preucil never explained why he asked him to make the call, nor its reason.

Povolvy could give the investigators no further information about Preucil and his activities, but it was clear he had been used for the telephone call.

Josef Kotnik

The investigators became aware of a man called Josef Kotnik. He accused Augustin Preucil of assaulting him in Benešov on 18 July 1944.

The reasons for this assault were unclear, but in a statement, Kotnik claimed that while on a tram at the terminus in Branik, he was 'brutally assaulted' by Preucil. The police arrived and Preucil was rude towards the officers, threatening them with the Gestapo and being taken to the Petschek Palace. He refused to identify himself to the police and only identified himself once they arrived at the Josefska police station in Prague. Once he had calmed down, Preucil told the officers that he had not identified himself as he was an agent of the German State Police.

The reason for the assault is unclear and the post-war investigators were more concerned with Preucil's Gestapo comments and threats. What was apparent was his willingness to use violence and threats to anyone who got in his way. As we have already seen, he was quick to pull out a gun and threatened a friend, he discussed with Max Brantal the shooting of Gerik and Čurda; and he was quick to remove any opposition.

Josek Kotnik was not the only person to have complained to the police about Augustin Preucil. After the war, Jaroslava Vancurova approached the Czechoslovakian police in May 1945 with a complaint about Preucil, which was soon passed on to the investigation team.

Jaroslava Vancurova

On 4 May 1945 she made the following statement (it does not translate into perfect English):

> On April 12th 1945, I was released from the penitentiary in Aichach in Bavaria. When I arrived in Prague on April 15th 1945, and when I wanted to go to my apartment in 15 Chechova Street, Prague XIX, I found that a Gustav Preucil lived in my apartment according to the business card on the door.

Then I went looking for a place to my brother-in-law Oldrich Ukaur, with whom I still live at Bohumil Hajko's home in Prague.

I later found out that all my property had been confiscated by Inspector Kain (Gestapo) and that Mr Preucil had moved in there. He had moved out a few days ago, this was unknown until he handed over the keys to the apartment to someone.

About fourteen days ago, Inspector Hajn took away the furnishings of this one-room apartment, all my linen, suits, costumes, hats, fur coats, books, shoes and jewellery, such as a gold ladies' double watch, two gold rings and several gold brooches from Breddovska Street, I suffered a total loss of 100,000 kr. I also note that in 1943, I was sentenced to only two years without confiscation of property and other punishments.

A further statement was made to police on 25 May 1945:

On May 4th 1945, I reported the theft of my apartment in Prague to the police. The theft was committed by Gestapo men Heim and Preucil. I couldn't inspect the apartment, because Preucil had the keys to the apartment and was outside of Prague. Today, I had the apartment opened-up, I found one envelope with the name Augustin Preucil on it and a note that I am attaching. Based on these found things, I conclude that Preucil was either a member of the Gestapo or worked for the Gestapo.

It was clear that the apartment was given to a Gestapo agent for his own use. As previously stated, the Gestapo often confiscated properties which they regularly used in operations or as safe houses for confidents. This small, but significant piece of evidence was one of the final pieces of the jigsaw, it was clear Augustin Preucil was a Gestapo agent.

Chapter Eleven

Girlfriends and family

Despite having a young wife in Sunderland, it soon became clear that Augustin Preucil was not concerned about adultery. We have already seen that he was very close to Milena Tomanova – how close is open to debate, but he was also emotionally attached to at least two other women between 1939 and 1945. These women were Ella Fortikova and Jirina Vanisova.

Jirina Vanisova

The relationship with Jirina Vanisova was one that would again display the menace in Augustin Preucil's character, as well as the shadow of his Gestapo employers.

Vanisova had known Preucil for two years by the time she spoke to the Czechoslovakian investigators. She told them that she knew he had been arrested by the Gestapo at the end of 1943 and imprisoned in Terezín concentration camp, being released in May 1944. Since they met in May 1944, she claimed to have been in love with him.

Vanisova explained that Preucil had confided in her that, in the summer of 1939, he had been secretly sent from the Protectorate of Plzen to fight abroad with the Free Czech Air Force. He had gone to France and then on to England.

Although she had asked him a number of times, he never fully explained how he had returned to Czechoslovakia. On one occasion, he told her he had been employed with the Fa Rolny company in France after having previously worked for them in Prague. Preucil said the company collapsed after the German invasion of France and he had returned to Prague with the other Czechoslovakian employees.

Later, Preucil changed the account he gave Vanisova, stating that he had come from England with 'some purpose' that would not benefit the Germans. The Germans had persecuted him since he arrived and imprisoned him in Terezín, but he never explained this in detail.

Vanisova told the investigators that whenever she tried to clarify his return and question his arrival in Czechoslovakia, he would just say that he could not tell her the true story, as he feared the Gestapo would also arrest her. He told her that the Gestapo knew about his contacts and his relationship with her. If they detained her, they would give her injections which would control her thoughts and she could tell them everything about him. For this reason, he could not tell her too much about his mission and this would protect her.

Vanisova said Preucil was always very nervous and constantly in fear of the Germans watching and persecuting him. He told her that he was often summoned to the Petschek Palace where the Gestapo would interrogate him, but he never disclosed what they asked him. She pushed him and eventually, on one occasion, he did disclose that the Gestapo still wanted to know the purpose of his return to Czechoslovakia.

Preucil never once said anything about working for the Gestapo to Vanisova. On the contrary, he always claimed that he was working against the Germans and he was fearful that after his experience in Terezín, they would 'remove him for good'.

Preucil was so nervous, he even suspected those whose reliability Vanisova did not doubt. She told the investigators that her family once gave temporary accommodation to a Czechoslovakian family called Schnitd, but Preucil immediately believed them to be Gestapo agents whose purpose was to observe him.

Preucil had told her about his friend Max Brantal and their time together in the air force, but he claimed Max had been called in by the Gestapo in Prague and ordered to spy upon him. He only knew this because of Max's suspicious questions, so they were no longer friends and Preucil claimed to have stopped all contact with him.

At the end of January or the beginning of February 1945, Vanisova received a letter from a man called Preizler who lived in Zbraslav. He was a German, who said he had seen her on the train from Prague to Zbraslav and would like to get to know her. She brought the letter to the attention of Preucil and told him that she had not been using that train, in fact, she was travelling between Braslava and Prague. Preucil instantly said he believed this man Preizler to be another Gestapo agent and was spying on them.

Vanisova wanted to destroy the letter and forget the matter, but Preucil took it away and said he would investigate him.

The Czech investigators showed Jirina Vanisova an exhibited letter, signed in the name of Jan Preizler. She told them the letter was identical to the once she had received and Preucil had taken away. There were notes scribbled on the envelope of the letter and these were in the handwriting of Preucil.

The letter was poor in terms of spelling and Preucil justified his suspicion of Preizler to Vanisova, by pointing out the number of mistakes in the text of the letter.

Vanisova said that in the final hours of the German occupation, Preucil was fearful of the Germans and would not sleep at his parents' home in Mechenice. He therefore stayed at the Vanisova home in Chvozhnice.

Vanisova told the investigators that she never had any dealings with the Gestapo and she could not recall Preucil having any large sums of money at his disposal. In fact, she thought he dressed modestly and his spending was in no way out of the ordinary.

She claimed that Preucil did not work after his release from Terezín, but laboured for his parents on their farm. The Gestapo made him work however, giving him a clerical job at the Veletrzny Palace in Prague. Preucil told her he hated the job and had to get out again.

Vanisova recalled Preucil obtaining a medical certificate, sometime in the winter of 1944–45, the doctor stating he could not work due to his nervous disposition.

Vanisova added that Preucil was very nervous and once told her that his former lover, Ella Fortikova, had probably turned him in to the Gestapo. This, he claimed, was because she had known he wanted to go abroad in 1939.

Vanisova did not recall ever seeing any German documents in his possession, but Preucil once showed her an envelope bearing a German stamp. He told her it was another Gestapo letter summoning him for further questioning and although she did not speak or read German, it looked like it could have been a summons.

In March 1945, Preucil was in a deep state of depression when he was summoned by the Gestapo once again. He became very angry and said he would take a revolver with him to the Petschek Palace and deal with them personally. (Clearly this did not happen.)

On another occasion, Vanisova had been with Preucil in the Vagon restaurant in Prague when he pointed out a well-dressed man. Preucil claimed the man was watching them and that he never got any peace from the constant Gestapo surveillance. As a result, Preucil quickly paid the bill and they left the restaurant, he called the man Gestapo Hajk, but Vanisova did not know him or his real name. She also added that she did not know Max Brantal when the investigators asked about him.

Jirina Vanisova's evidence portrayed a nervous and agitated Preucil, someone who, in 1944 and 1945, knew his betrayal would soon catch up with him.

Jan Preizler

The Czech investigation team located the man who wrote the letter to Jirina Vanisova. Jan Preizler had attended the German school in Krausevych Boudy and also a Czech school. He told the investigators that he could read and write, but he made a lot of spelling mistakes. He told them that he did not know Preucil and this was the first time he had ever heard the name. He also added that he did not know Jirina Vanisova personally.

Preizler admitted that in December 1944, possibly January 1945, he heard from a friend called Alois Vesel about a good-looking girl called Jirina Vanisova. His friend drew his attention to her as a suitable woman for him, so he got her address (he did not say how) and wrote to her, describing his personal circumstances and his desire to meet with her.

Preizler never received a reply, but when he inquired via Jirina Tumove, a worker in Hvozdnice who knew Vanisova, he learnt she was not interested in him.

He told the investigators that he was employed during the German occupation as a mechanic at the Klevin company in Modrany. He had no contact at all with the German security apparatus, especially the Gestapo. He had never been stopped or questioned by them or any other Germans.

He confirmed to the investigators that he had received no order from anyone to observe Preucil, and so he had never carried out such an act. Neither did he observe Jirina Vanisova, all he wanted to do was meet her. When he wrote that he had seen her on the train, this was not true and was just an excuse to justify his initial approach and letter.

Finally, Preizler was shown the exhibited letter shown to Jirina Vanisova and he confirmed it was the letter written by him and sent to Vanisova.

Ella Fortikova

Ella Fortikova was a former girlfriend of Preucil. He thought she had reported him to the Gestapo, so it was imperative the Czech investigators located and interviewed her quickly.

Once located, Ella told the investigators that she had known Preucil for quite some time. They had met when they were both employed by the Rolny company in Vodickova Street, Prague. She said they started an intimate relationship just after the establishment of the Protectorate and that he told her about Czech airmen being transported across the border to continue the fight against the Germans.

One day, Preucil disappeared and she had no idea where he had gone. After some time, she received two notes, one from Denmark and another from France. Neither note contained any real information, other than greetings from Preucil, and she later discovered that he had fled abroad.

In 1941 or 1942, Ella was working at the Prisak store in Prague when Preucil suddenly entered the shop. He told her he was a now parachutist and had been dropped by the English intelligence services to carry out an important mission against the Germans. When he was dropped, he had suffered an injury above his eye which had left a scar.

Despite his return to Prague, Ella claimed to have only seen him two or three times. He did not disclose any details about how he had returned to the country, nor whether the Germans knew of his presence.

On one of the few occasions they met, he pulled out a revolver and told Ella that he must shoot himself immediately if the Germans were to capture him. After this, she did not see him for several months.

When Preucil reappeared, Ella noticed that he was 'moving quite freely' and without any apparent worries. He told her that he had saved the entire family of a businessman in Dejvice from the Gestapo (the Tomanova family). He then added that he was dating the businessman's daughter. However, despite his claims, Ella said she started to date him again after this meeting. They would often meet with his friends Max Brantal and Milan Hajke at the Vagon restaurant in the Metro, Prague. (Milan Hajke clearly being the alleged Gestapo man Jirina Vanisova mentioned when they had attended the same restaurant.)

Ella recalled that Preucil was always making anti-German comments and took an anti-German stance, while still claiming to her that he worked for the English intelligence service.

On 21 January 1943, in order to avoid conscription and being deployed on work away from Prague by the Germans, Ella joined the local police as a telephone switchboard operator. This allegedly caused some concern to Preucil.

In the autumn of 1943, Preucil was arrested by the Gestapo and taken to Terezín. He was released in the spring of 1944, but Ella said he didn't disclose the reason for his arrest, later claiming he had been arrested due to information from her uncle, Ladislava Svaska. Ella totally dismissed this allegation, as her uncle worked for the underground movement and 'He would never do this to her lover.' She totally refuted the allegation and told Preucil she was not responsible either. Despite this, Ella felt Preucil clearly suspected her because of her new role at the police station.

Ella told the investigators that she had defended herself so robustly, that a rift developed between the two of them and their relationship ended. She told Preucil his claims were unfair and he was a rogue, but he suddenly claimed that the Germans had treated him very well in Terezín and they had done a lot for him. He now 'felt for them', and would work with them. Preucil then added that if he had been caught by the Germans earlier, they would have shot him, but these men treated him 'wonderfully'. Ella said she was shocked and disgusted by his outburst and had told him to shoot himself if he had any honour left in his body.

Ella said Preucil had bought her a beret and some other items which had cost 1,500 Koruna. After they split up, she sent him the cost of the items via a postal order.

The investigators asked Ella about Preucil's assertion that she had deliberately become pregnant. She again stated that they had an intimate relationship, but she didn't get pregnant and would never do such a thing to him – even if it was to get help or money.

Ella said Preucil had tried to rekindle the relationship and claimed he loved her. He asked her to go to his apartment, but when she refused, he threatened to destroy her and her whole family. He claimed she might be Gestapo, but then added she listened to foreign radio broadcasts and made anti-German speeches in front of him. Despite his threats, she insisted the relationship was at an end and he left. She did not see him again.

She told the investigators that while Preucil was in Terezín prison, his mother came to the Fortikova home. His mother claimed she knew they were a good family and that was why she did not want Ella to marry her son. She said her son was working with the Germans and she was very upset about this.

The investigators confronted Ella in the interview room with Preucil. Ella according to the records, immediately stated:

You, told me after your release from Terezín that the Germans treated you decently, that others would have shot you, that you sympathised with the Germans and that you would work with them. You threatened to destroy me and my family if I didn't visit your apartment.

Preucil replied:

These statements are not true. I did not threaten the witness or her family. I did show friendly feelings towards Germans, on the contrary, I did not trust the witness, because the Gestapo claimed to me that I was betrayed and arrested as a result of the witness' report. Sometime after my dismissal, the witness demanded the sum of 10,000–15,000 kr. From me for reasons of friendship, because she is in a different state and wants to get help. I gave her 1,500 kr. I note that it was the summer of 1944 and the last intimate contact I had with the witness was before my arrest, i.e. November 2nd, 1943. She was therefore pregnant in the summer of 1944, so not from me. I gave her the money anyway.

Ella responded:

He invented this. I never received cash from him and I sent him the 1,500 kr. For the hat and cork shoes.

It was clear to the investigation team, there was a lot of animosity between Ella Fortikova and Augustin Preucil. It was also now clear that the man had little honour, having a young wife in Sunderland and yet having affairs with Ella Fortikova, Milena Tomanova and Jirina Vanisova.

Marie Preucil

Marie Preucil, the mother of the accused, was also interviewed by the Czech investigation team. She had recently been treated for anxiety, but claimed to have recovered and was fit to be interviewed and give evidence.

She told the investigators that her son had gone abroad in the summer of 1939 and returned to Czechoslovakia in September 1941. She had asked him how he had got home, but he refused to answer her questions, with the justification that the Germans would eliminate him and the family if they knew the truth.

He stayed with his parents in Trebsin and moved with them to Mechenice when the village became an SS training area. She claimed he was always anti-German and displayed strong anglophile feelings to his family.

On one occasion, his mother claimed Augustin brought 100,000 Koruna to the family home. He said the Germans had forced him to take it and speak on the public radio. He said, he had refused to talk on the radio and added that he would never speak against the republic, even if it cost the family their lives. Marie said she had told Augustin not to take her life into consideration, and that his parents were willing to make the greatest of sacrifices.

Marie Preucil said she had wanted to burn the money, but her son kept it separate and later told her he had used it to assist the Tomanova family in Prague. She was ashamed of this money and did not take one penny of it from him.

In November 1943, Augustin was arrested and sent to Terezín prison. Marie claimed she initially did not know where he was, but his girlfriend Ella Fortikova had told her about his arrest and location. She claimed Ella had come to Mechenice after he was detained and introduced herself to his mother. Ella brought some flour with her as a gift (which was rationed at the time) and they talked.

Preucil's mother told the investigators that she later visited Ella's home twice, taking money to buy her a goose and then an egg. She had asked Ella about her future with Augustin, but denied ever telling the girl not to marry her son or saying he had joined the Germans.

Marie told the investigators she knew nothing about her son working for the Germans. However, when he was released from Terezín a letter arrived at the family home summoning him to the Gestapo headquarters. Her son told her he would not attend, but he was always afraid of the Germans and believed they were pursuing him.

In 1944, the Gestapo summoned Marie to their headquarters and interrogated her about her son's contacts. They ordered her, upon pain of death, to report where he worked and who he met. Despite their command, she told Augustin about her summons and interrogation. She also learned that a friend of Augustin's, Max Brantal, had also been summoned and given the same order to watch and report his actions.

Marie said this strain caused her nervous tension and she collapsed and had to undergo prolonged treatment at the

Bulovka hospital in Prague. Augustin also suffered with his mental health, he too was very nervous and felt he was being pushed around, and pushed hard, by the Germans.

Marie concluded by stating that after the war ended, Augustin was arrested in Mechenice and the family home was searched by the Czechoslovakian authorities. She added that she never found out how he had got from England back to Czechoslovakia.

It is hard to know who to believe with Ella Fortikova and Marie Preucil. They both had a vested interest in Augustin Preucil, his mother clearly wanted to save him, but what was the intention of Ella?

Chapter Twelve

Czech and RAFVR evidence

Augustin Preucil had tried to baffle the investigators concerning his activities with the Gestapo and the Czech airmen in the United Kingdom. In addition, he had given varied accounts of his contact with the SOE traitors – Čurda, Gerik, Kindl and Grabovsky; but he knew he would have problems explaining his contacts with captured Czechoslovakian aircrew in Prague. It is therefore hardly surprising, the only contact he mentioned in his interrogation, was that with František Burda. As the two men already knew one another, Preucil had to give an account and a reason for their meeting in the Gestapo headquarters.

As previously mentioned, Czechoslovakian airmen were deemed by the Nazis to be citizens of the Greater Reich, as residents of the Protectorate of Bohemia and Moravia. Any Czechoslovakian joining the Royal Air Force Volunteer Reserve (RAFVR) would therefore be deemed a traitor and could expect a death sentence.

The first Czechoslovakian airmen captured by the Germans in September 1940 were treated as traitors and expected a firing squad. The crew from 311 (Czech) Squadron who had been flying a Vickers Wellington when it was shot down were initially sent to the Dulug Luft camp at Oberursel, but a warrant was issued on 28 September and they were sent to the Berlin-Alt

Moatbit prison, and then on to Tegal prison. The fear of capture was so high for Czech airmen, the radio operator from this aircraft, Sergeant Karel Kunka, shot himself with his service revolver rather than surrender. He died of his wounds a day later. Like many others, he feared probable torture, execution and repercussions for his family back in Czechoslovakia.

For the rest of his crew, a trial date was set for the 18 February 1941, at the Reich War Court in Berlin; but this was suddenly adjourned and the men were sent to a prisoner of war camp. It is said the British government had made representations through the Swiss Red Cross, that severe retaliatory measures would be taken if the Czechoslovakian airmen were harmed.

Over the next three years a significant number of Czech aircrew were captured and sent to various prisoner camps.

In the summer of 1944, the Department for National Security made a final attempt to deal with the 'Czech perpetrators of high treason'. Twenty-five Czechoslovakian airmen were selected from the various PoW camps and transported to the Gestapo headquarters in Prague for questioning. The men were to go on trial at the Reich War Court and an intimated death sentence was given for each man.

The British once again made representations that this was a breach of the Geneva Convention and illegal. Suddenly and unexpectedly, the Reich Military Attorney's office quietly terminated the cases with the proviso the hearing should take place after the war – a war the Nazis had all but lost by the end of 1944.

Unfortunately, the Gestapo destroyed the vast majority of their records as the war concluded. They spent a number of days with human hostages in their Prague headquarters, before silently leaving for Germany. Many Gestapo officers managed to get to Germany, but others were killed before they could be interrogated and Preucil's collaboration discovered from the lips of those who employed him.

However, despite a lack of direct senior level Gestapo evidence, there were a number of Czechoslovakian airmen who remembered Preucil very clearly, both from before the war and his actions during their imprisonment in Prague by the Nazis.

On 28 August 1945, a (translated) report from Czechoslovakian Air Force Command to the Field Court of the First Bench at LC Army Corps stated:

> At your request, specifically during the oral interview, we send you the case against Preucil and allegations made by Major Rejthar, Captain [Flight Lieutenant] Burda, Sergeant Sichrovský... [In a note from the Air Ministry (AM) dated 14/3/1942, he was declared dead according to AM regulations.]
>
> Flight Sergeant Augustin Preucil 787344 born 3/7/1914 in Trebsin, was missing on 18/9/1941 with a 'Hurricane' type of aircraft on a training flight from 55 OTU RAF Usworth.
>
> On September 18, 1941 at 6.15pm, Preucil landed with an undamaged Hurricane on the territory of Belgium, where he fled into the forest after landing. The next morning, he came out of the forest and surrendered to the German guards, who were looking for him in the area. [Description from AM]

By meeting the returnees and captives, it was found: In the spring of 1944, he met Captain Burda in the Petschek Palace, where he appeared freely in an impeccable civilian suit and addressed Captain Burda, 'Lieutenant what are you doing here?' – he was very nervous. He offered a cigarette to Burda and said, 'You remember Chartres, I, Standera, Stehlik was with your squadron,' to which he added, 'I'm as nervous as a pig.' [Sergeant Zdeněk Josef Sichrovský was the navigator on another 311 Squadron Wellington shot down near Tilburg, Holland, at 23.17 hours on 17 January 1942. He was injured and taken to hospital where this questioning took place.]

In July 1942, Sergeant Sichrovský was interrogated in a hospital in Berlin by a German intelligence officer who, among other things, asked if he knew Preucil. After a positive answer, the intelligence officer recounted that Preucil had landed in The Netherlands with the newest, intact airplane of the time – the Hurricane – and that he had declared, 'That he would not work for the Jews and that he was enlisting in the services of Germany.'

Sergeant Preucil was a pilot in 1938 at the training squadron let.pl 4 in Prague. Recently, before his disappearance, he was supposed to be court martialled for air misconduct. There is no news about its reliability. After March 15 1939, he opened a suit shop in Vinohradske in Prague.

Personality: talkative, boastful, like to talk about flying, liar, coward.

In just a few paragraphs the report insinuated that the man could not be trusted, was a coward and a traitor.

How many airmen came into contact with Augustin Preucil at the Gestapo headquarters is unclear, the main witness who gave evidence to the investigators was Captain Flight Lieutenant František Burda. However, there were others including Flight Lieutenant Ivo Tonder and Flight Sergeant Viliam Bufka. Others including Petr Uruba and Flying Officer Jaroslav Zafouk almost certainly came into contact with Preucil.

We shall look at the comments and evidence of these men in a moment, but first there were officers who would give evidence of Preucil's actions before his flight from Britain.

Major Stanislav Rejthar

Major Rejthar told the investigators that he knew Augustin Preucil in France, where they had served together at Chartres air base, in January 1940 until the beginning of April 1940.

Preucil had been in another squadron at the time, but Rejthar said he had heard only bad things about him, especially from (Sergeant) Zima, who suggested he should be 'kicked-out' of the air force for gross indiscipline. This was because Preucil was damaging the good name of Czechoslovakian pilots in France. Later, Zima would also express disbelief at the activities of Preucil.

After the fall of France, Rejthar saw Preucil again at the Czech depot at RAF Cosford in England. He later heard about Preucil's marriage to an English girl and a letter he had written to the Aviation Inspectorate in London, in which he requested support in an unusual form. (This is believed to have been for a collection of money to support his wedding to Muriel in Sunderland.)

Major Rejthar told the investigators that he later read a confidential document, this detailed the fact Preucil had flown from England to the enemy. He said the news had caused great indignation among Czech pilots, the whole matter was discussed so secretly at the time, he did not know the full circumstances surrounding Preucil's departure to Belgium.

Major Rejthar added that during a recent visit to London, Lieutenant Colonel Kordula from the Czech Aviation Inspectorate, asked whether Preucil had been detained in Czechoslovakia. During a conversation Kordula drew Rejthar's attention to a report sent to the Czech Ministry of National Defence (MNO) in London concerning Preucil's flight. This report had been forwarded to the OBZ – the air force headquarters and was in the possession of the post-war investigators.

Captain Rudolf Zima

Captain Zima gave his account to the investigators and confirmed that he too had known Augustin Preucil from their time at Chartres airfield near Paris in 1939. He had been a flying instructor, but he had also met Preucil in Paris before they went to Chartres, that was around August 1939. At the time, Zima and Preucil had both signed a formal commitment to join the

French Foreign legion, but they never served in the legion and were later transferred to the French Air Force.

On the 5 October 1939, the two men were sent to Chartres to start training and Zima was Preucil's flying instructor.

At the time, Zima was a sergeant like Preucil and the two men would regularly chat. Preucil had told him at Chartres that he had been employed by a clothing company in Prague. He had set up his own shop in the city and ended up with a debt of 50,000 Koruna. Preucil therefore decided to flee abroad to escape his debts.

Zima said Preucil had never said anything to him about the Gestapo allowing him to cross the Polish border and report back to them.

Zima recalled that Augustin Preucil was undisciplined and careless. He showed no apparent interest in the service and was generally a very poor pilot.

On 10 May 1940, Zima was still at Chartres when the Germans attacked France. He formed part of a local defence force for the airfield, but was injured and admitted to a hospital. As the other Czech pilots withdrew and headed for England, Zima discharged himself from the hospital and managed to get to a port and a ship bound for England.

When they arrived in England in July 1940, Zima was sent to 310 (Czech) Squadron, where he said he denounced the 'nature and ignorance' of Preucil and did not recommend him as a fellow squadron pilot. This, he claimed, was purely for the best interests of the service.

Zima recalled hearing that Preucil had circulated a note requesting other Czech pilots organise a collection for him, as he was getting married and needed the money. He then heard that before going missing, he should have been prosecuted by an English court-martial for aviation misconduct. In late 1941, Zima heard the news that Preucil had taken a plane and flown to mainland Europe.

In October 1942, Zima was assigned to the RAF in Canada as a flying instructor. He recalled that during a business trip to Washington, USA, in April 1945, he visited the Czech Embassy and spoke with Colonel Alexander Hesse who knew Augustin Preucil. Hesse told him that Preucil had fled on purpose, landed in The Netherlands or Belgium, and that the civilian population had assisted and concealed him. However, Preucil betrayed them to the Germans who executed a number of the civilians.

At the end of May 1945, Zima met Captain František Burda at RAF Cosford. Burda had just returned from captivity in Germany, but he recalled being transported to Pankrác Prison in Prague in 1944. He had told Zima he had been approached by Preucil who greeted him as a friend in the presence of the Gestapo, but Burda told the Germans, he did not know him.

Captain Jaroslav Bella

Captain Bella told the investigators he did not know Preucil personally. He had been abroad from 1939 and was in England in 1940. He knew from work at the Aviation Inspectorate in London, that Preucil had not returned from a flight in 1941. He also knew the English intelligence service had informed them that he had landed in Belgium or The Netherlands and betrayed the civilians who helped him hide from the Germans.

Captain Karel Šifner

Captain Šifner stated that in 1941 he was attached to the Czech Ministry of National Defence (MNO) in London. He had known Preucil and knew from reports that he had not returned from a training flight in September 1941. Preucil was listed as missing, but over time, it soon emerged he had flown to Europe and was in the Protectorate of Bohemia and Moravia.

English officers had informed Šifner that according to intelligence reports, Preucil was in the service of the Gestapo in the Protectorate; this was later confirmed when captured Czech airmen returned after the war.

Šifner added that he had spoken to a number of returning Czech prisoners, but he could not remember specific names. They all stated Augustin Preucil was with the Gestapo at their headquarters in Prague. In each case, Preucil had spoken to the Czechoslovakian airmen in the presence of Gestapo officials and guards.

Sergeant Zdeněk Josef Sichrovský

It was claimed that Sergeant Sichrovský provided a statement, but nothing can be found in the case files in the Czech Regional Archives in Prague. He was the airman who was hospitalised in Berlin and during his interrogation, the Luftwaffe intelligence officer had mentioned Preucil by name.

Captain (Flight Lieutenant) František Burda

Captain Burda told the investigators that he got to know Preucil when he was in France and they were in the same unit for about seven months. Burda had the impression that Preucil was a reckless man, who indulged in regular card games and upset the rest of the team with his poor behaviour and discipline.

When they transferred to England in the summer of 1940 Burda did not see Preucil again, so he could not personally comment of the circumstances of his departure to Belgium the following year.

Burda had trained as a pilot at Prostejov in October 1937, but this was a year after Preucil had attended the flying school. In June 1938, he joined the 40th Squadron as part of the 4th Air Regiment. When the unit was demobilised, he fled to Ostrave where he assisted the underground movement. They smuggled Burda on to a train to Poland and he was sent to the camp at Bronowice Male. It is likely he met Augustin Preucil there, as both men were sent to the port of Gydnia and on to France, on board the Swedish ship *Kastelholm*, which arrived in France in late August 1939.

Burda, like Preucil, had to enlist in the French Foreign Legion before finally joining the French Air Force and training at Chartres. He recalled recommending that Preucil be expelled from the air force as a result of his poor behaviour, which he claimed was both personal and criminal – although he did not go into detail in his evidence. He said Preucil gave the impression of being a reckless person who undermined discipline within the unit by not fulfilling his duties.

After they had both moved to England, a fellow Czech officer told Burda that Preucil was in debt and led a 'disorderly' life.

Burda must have been a better pilot, or perhaps he applied himself more than Preucil, because while Preucil continued his training, Burda flew combat missions with the French unit GC I/4. He shot down a Messerschmitt 109E in June 1940, before travelling to Casablanca and Gibraltar. He then went by ship to Liverpool, arriving a few days after Preucil, and was sent to RAF Cosford.

(The two men joined the RAFVR on 24 July 1940, Burda being commissioned, before they were sent to 6 OTU at Sutton Bridge to convert to Hurricanes. On the 7 October 1940, Preucil joined 43 Squadron at Usworth, while Burda went to 310 (Czech) Squadron at Duxford. Why Preucil went to 43 Squadron and Burda joined a dedicated Czech squadron is unclear, but Preucil may have been in need of further training and was sent to the 'resting and re-equipping' 43 Squadron, while Burda went to a front-line unit. However, there is also the possibility that the RAF and intelligence services were still checking Preucil's background, not to mention any Czechoslovakian reports about his previous indiscipline.)

On 27 February 1943, Burda was shot down while escorting American B-24 Liberator bombers over France. He baled-out and was captured and interrogated before being sent to the infamous Stalag Luft III in Sagan.

At the beginning of August 1944, Burda was sent to Prague for interrogation by the Gestapo as part of the twenty-five Czechoslovakian PoWs sent for questioning as traitors to the Greater Reich and the Protectorate of Bohemia and Moravia.

While being held at the Gestapo headquarters and questioned, Burda remembered one morning, at about 10.00 hours, the door to his cell was opened and Preucil came rushing into the room. Preucil clearly recognised Burda and asked how he was and what he was doing there. He even offered him a cigarette. Burda said Preucil moved around quite easily and started chatting in a friendly manner to the escorting Gestapo officer, who had been listening to their conversation. The officer spoke with Preucil and Burda heard Preucil tell him in Czechoslovakian that Burda had been in Poland and France. The meeting concluded and Preucil departed.

After his interrogation ended, Burda was taken back to Pankrác Prison and later moved to the infamous Colditz Castle near Leipzig. In 1945, Burda was finally liberated by the US Army before returning to Britain where he reported his contact with Preucil.

Burda told the post-war investigators that the distance from Sunderland (RAF Usworth) to Preucil's place of landing in Belgium, was about 350 miles and would be about two and a half hours flying time. A Hawker Hurricane with full fuel tanks would have made that journey in that time, if he flew straight and did not stray from his flight-path.

Flight Sergeant Viliam Bufka

Flight Sergeant Bufka was the sole survivor of a 311 Squadron Vickers Wellington shot down on 23 June 1941. He fractured his leg and after treatment was sent to a prison camp.

Like many others, in the summer of 1944 he was transferred to the Gestapo headquarters in Prague for prosecution as a traitor. He claimed he was 'greeted' by Preucil in the Gestapo headquarters and the two men chatted in a cell. When Preucil left him, he heard him telling the attendant Gestapo officer what had been discussed.

Captain Petr Urubu

Captain Urubu was the pilot of another 311 Squadron Wellington which landed accidentally in France on the night of 5/6 February 1941. He was sent to the Gestapo in Prague, where he later recalled meeting with Viliam Bufka. The two men tried to talk, but the Gestapo yelled abuse at them and prevented them from speaking to one another.

Although Urubu never mentioned actual contact with Preucil, it is highly likely that he did meet him, bearing in mind he was there at the same time Bufka had spoken to Preucil. It is not known whether he was approached by the Czech investigators.

Captain (Flight Lieutenant) Ivo Tonder

Captain Tonder followed a similar route to the other Czech pilots via France to the United Kingdom in 1940. He joined 312 (Czech) Squadron in late October 1940 and served with them until 3 June 1942, when he was shot down and captured.

Tonder does not feature in the Court file of those who came into contact with Preucil in 1944, but he was held by the Gestapo in Prague and had apparently come into contact with him.

On 25 March 1944, he was one of the so-called 'Great Escapers' who tunnelled out of Stalag Luft III in Sagan. Unfortunately, along with some British RAF officers, he was recaptured on 28 March 1944 and taken to Liberec in Czechoslovakia. His fellow RAF officers were murdered by the Gestapo, but as a Czech he was sent to join his compatriot airmen in Prague on 16 April 1944. He was held by the Gestapo until the end of November when he was sent to the prison camp at Barth and then on to Colditz.

In recent years Ivo Tonder in the book *In the Heavens and in Hell*, recalled being interrogated at the Prague Gestapo headquarters after his recapture. He remembered meeting a Czech pilot in the Gestapo building, who got himself into trouble with a stolen 'Spitfire' which he flew back to the Nazis. Although Tonder never named the man in the book, they had been on the same ship when they left France in 1940 and they knew one another very well.

Tonder expected the pilot to expose his history, but this man – clearly Augustin Preucil – told the Gestapo officer he had never seen Tonder before in his life. Ivo Tonder said this man had betrayed so many others, but he didn't betray him (possibly because of their earlier friendship).

Author Simon Pearson in his book *The Great Escaper: The Life and Death of Roger Bushell* (who was 'Big X' as portrayed by Richard Attenborough in the movie *The Great Escape*) writes that Bushell was captured on 19 May 1942 in Prague with Czech Pilot Officer Jaroslav Zafouk.

The two men had escaped in 1941 and headed to Prague, believing they could get assistance from Zafouk's family. They were lodged with the Zeithammel family, but were betrayed and captured in a Gestapo raid. As we have seen, Viliam Gerik had recently been captured and the Gestapo were expecting the arrival of further SOE parachutists. Initially, Bushell and Zafouk were believed to be parachutists or British intelligence agents.

The airmen were taken to the 'cinema room' in the Petschek Palace, where prisoners sat on benches looking at a plain whitewashed wall. They awaited interrogation, while prisoners in an adjacent room were questioned, with torture often being inflicted. Eventually, they would be placed in the small, poorly lit former vaults, which now served as cells. The cells measured 12ft high, 8ft long and just 4ft wide, with a hard wooden bed. This is what all visitors to the Petschek Palace experienced, including Preucil in September 1941.

Simon Pearson states that post-war, Ivo Tonder told British investigators that he was interrogated by a Gestapo man called Bauer, a tall, thin, blonde-haired man probably in his late forties. This was almost certainly Bedřich Bauer who worked with Oskar Fleischer and allegedly took control of Preucil towards the end of the war.

Jaroslav Zafouk was also interrogated by Bedřich Bauer, which prompts the question: was Preucil involved in these interrogations? If Bauer was the man dealing with Bushell and Zafouk, and Preucil was assisting with Gerik, it is highly likely he was involved with speaking to Zafouk and possibly even Bushell. He was certainly in and around the Gestapo building in May and June 1942.

Zafouk was held for several weeks and is said to have been beaten and tortured by the Gestapo; Roger Bushell, however, was sent to Stalag Luft III at Sagan after a few days, where he took part in The Great Escape.

In terms of a timeline, it is possible the treacherous Czech pilot who was controlled by Oskar Fleischer, took a part in these interrogations:

- Police Station Commander Němec in his evidence, stated Preucil was absent from Trebsin during May and June 1942.
- Viliam Gerik had been detained on 4 April 1942 and started to assist the Gestapo. He appears to have told them about incoming Czech SOE parachutists and radio codes.
- Both Preucil and Viliam Gerik admitted meeting one another in April 1942 at the Petschek Palace (in the company of the Gestapo's Oskar Fleischer).
- On 12 May 1942 the Gestapo had intercepted a Czech SOE radio message which mentioned preparations to assassinate 'H'. They feared reprisals.
- The Zeithammel home was raided and the two airmen detained on 19 May 1942.
- During May–June 1942, both Bushell and Zafouk were interrogated by Bedřich Bauer at the Gestapo HQ.
- In late May 1942, Bushell, having apparently been suspected of being a British SIS agent, was sent to Stalag Luft III in Sagan, when the Gestapo was satisfied he was an escaped British pilot.
- Reinhard Heydrich was attacked on 27 May 1942 in Prague. He died on the 4 June.

- In June 1942, Karel Čurda surrendered himself to the Gestapo in Prague and met with Preucil.
- On 17 June 1942, the assassins and other Czech SOE men were killed at the church in Prague.

The evidence listed above is surely more than coincidental and Preucil must have been involved, not only in the interrogation of the Czech airmen in 1944, but also those in 1942. He was by his own admission at the Gestapo headquarters and meeting SOE parachutists in April–June 1942. He was also allegedly asked to speak to Czech airmen in England via a radio broadcast, so why would his Gestapo masters have not utilised him at a time when they expected significant SOE/Resistance activity?

The following men were named by Preucil during his interrogation by the Czech authorities, but they do not appear to have been approached or made statements about their dealings with him:

Squadron Leader Alexander Hess(e)

Squadron Leader Hess was a pre-war Czech pilot and escaped via Poland to France. He arrived in England in June 1940 and joined 310 (Czech) Squadron when it was formed in July 1940. He later went to the United States as the Czechoslovakian air attaché in 1942 and remained there, attempting to recruit expatriot Czech airmen. It is probably due to him being in the United States that the Czechoslovakian authorities did not interview him about Augustin Preucil.

It appears Preucil only came into contact with Hess at Chartres.

Major Jan Ambrus

Major Ambrus was the commanding officer of the Czechoslovakian Air Test Group in Prague in 1938, when the German occupation began. As a highly experienced pilot he would have been an asset to the Nazis, but he managed to escape via Yugoslavia to France and was based at Chartres in an administrative role.

He escaped again to England and was commissioned into the RAF Volunteer Reserve in July 1940, before converting to Hurricanes at No. 6 OTU and taking joint command of the new 312 (Czech) Squadron on 9 September 1940.

It is worth pausing to think that as a commanding officer, he would have some say in which Czech pilots joined his unit – and possibly he decided against Preucil due to his knowledge of the man.

Jan Ambrus joined the Czech Ministry of Defence in London during December 1940, before moving to the Czech Air Force Inspectorate in London in June 1941. As such, from Chartres to RAF Cosford and his roles in London, Ambrus would have known all about Preucil.

He was promoted to wing commander and went to Canada as air attaché in Ottawa, returning as a senior officer to Czechoslovakia after the war. In May 1946, he was a deputy in the Czech National Assembly. It is probably due to this position post war that he was not interviewed about Preucil, but his comments would have been very valuable to the investigation.

Captain/Major Josef Duda

Captain Duda started his pilot training in 1933 at Prostejov before becoming a fighter pilot. On the 8 June 1939, he escaped to Poland before travelling to France and training at Chartres airfield.

In May 1940 he joined French squadron GC II/5 and claimed two bombers destroyed, but with the retreat and defeat of France, he headed to Algeria. He then travelled via Gibraltar to Cardiff, arriving in August 1940.

Duda went to the Czech depot at Cosford before being commissioned and converting to Hurricanes at No. 6 OTU. He then joined 312 Squadron on the 5 September 1940.

After a period as a ferry pilot and an instructor in 1941, he joined the Czechoslovak Inspectorate General in London on 15 December 1941. In June 1943, he became a group captain and the Czech liaison officer at Bentley Priory, before taking command of the Czech Wing at RAF Manston in 1945.

After the war he remained in the Czech air force and was head of the flying school at Prostejov.

Why Preucil named Duda as a traitor and a Gestapo agent, and why he was never called to give evidence, is unclear to this day. It would not have been best practice for the Gestapo to reveal their sources' names, and it is more likely this was a fabrication of Preucil, possibly for some form of revenge. Had Duda and Preucil clashed while at Chartres or possibly at No. 6 OTU?

Sergeant Josef Stehlik

Sergeant Stehlik was a flying instructor when the German occupation began. He followed the well-trodden route to France and the airfield at Chartres near Paris in 1939. He was posted to a French fighter squadron and made a number of victory claims, before ending up at RAF Cosford and 312 Squadron on the 5 September 1940.

Stehlik became a flying instructor and was commissioned in August 1941, before going on to instruct in Canada. He remained in the Czech Air Force post war as a flying instructor and was in the country when Preucil was under investigation. Why he was not approached is again unknown.

Sergeant Miroslav Standera

Sergeant Standera was allegedly mentioned by Preucil when he met František Burda at the Gestapo headquarters.

Standera trained as an air force pilot in 1936, but fled to Poland on 1 June 1939. He went to France where, like many of his colleagues, he joined the French Foreign Legion. Like Preucil and other Czech pilots, he ended up at Chartres before joining a Czech group as part of the French Air Force.

In June 1940, he was seriously injured in combat with a Messerschmitt 109, but managed to escape to England. After recovering from his injuries, he mustered at RAF Cosford before converting to Hurricanes at 6 OTU at Sutton Bridge, where he probably met with Preucil once again. Eventually, he went to the second Czech fighter squadron, 312 (Czech) Squadron, in October 1940, while Preucil went to 43 Squadron at Usworth.

Standera flew operationally with 312 (Czech) Squadron until 1942, before becoming an instructor. He then rejoined 312 (Czech) Squadron. After completing his operational tour, he served as a flying instructor, before returning to 312 (Czech) Squadron for eight months. He also completed night-fighter training and served with 68 Squadron, having been commissioned. In August 1945, he returned to Czechoslovakia as a member of the air force flying de Havilland Mosquitos.

Why the investigators did not contact him is unknown, but they probably thought he was only a character witness.

Chapter Thirteen

Incriminating documents from the court file

The file in the Czech Regional Archives in Prague contains a number of documents that are both incriminating and fascinating to read. We have already covered some, but I shall consider others.

In the photographic plates within this book is an image of a document dated 23 June 1944 and signed by Augustin Preucil. The document declared in German the following:

PROMISE

According to s.2 ABS. 1 of the decree of the President of the State of March 8, 1940 SLG No.83.

I vow to obey the leader of the Greater German Reich Adolf Hitler, as the protector of the Protectorate of Bohemia and Moravia, to promote the interests of the Greater German Reich for the benefit of the Protectorate of Bohemia and Moravia, to follow the instructions of the head and government of the Protectorate of Bohemia and Moravia. To follow the morals, to observe the laws and to fulfil my official duties conscientiously.

The 23/6/1944
Augustin Preucil.

This is a damning document, clearly showing that Preucil had returned from Terezín concentration camp and taken an oath to work for the Nazis. It is highly likely he had signed a similar document in 1941, but this does not appear to have been recovered by the Czech authorities and was probably destroyed.

As we have seen, Preucil – while swearing allegiance to the Nazi regime – was working in an office covertly observing the Czech employees. Another document in the court file, gives details of his salary for this work (again translated):

Note

On the basis of the decree of the Ministry of Economy & Labour of 6/6/1944 No. P-1970 1/7/1944 (after consultation with Ref. SR Dr Nabak) in agreement with the Ministry of Finance decree of 25/5/1944 No.4400 44-VI/1 the following decree was made:

1. Date of birth: Augustin Preucil 7/3/1914
2. Education: elementary school 5 years and further education 4 and 2 years.
3. Marital status: Married.
4. Contract salary according to the analogy of the officials in the Chancellery auxiliary services, salary group III, salary level I.

Salary	11,520Kr
Activity fee	8,400Kr
Total	19,920Kr

7th of H. surcharge   1,404Kr
Total rounded   21,324Kr   **Signed……. Augustin Preucil.**

Subject: Regulation of contractual remuneration.

By the winter of 1944, the Nazis were losing the war and Preucil started to fear for his own future and safety. He therefore started to absent himself from the office.

On 28 December 1944, the following was sent to him:

Subject I – Administration

> Mr Augustin Preucil, contract employee:
> If you continue to be absent from work without giving a reason, you will be asked to report to work immediately or to submit a medical report by return mail. The illness, the probable duration of the same and the duration of the disability must be stated in the certificate. Entrusted with the conduct of the manager's business.

The Nazis system was as officious and efficient as ever and on 17 January 1945, Augustin Preucil sent in a letter of resignation to the Pensions Office.

A further report in the file sent to the Pensions Office states that his employment ceased on 28 February 1945.

Page 432 of the court case file contains a psychiatric report for Preucil dated 1 March 1945, from Dr Hofmeister of the Bulovka hospital (the same location that was treating his mother's illness.) The translated report states:

Diagnosis on admission: anxious depressive stage, probably of endogenous origin, equipped exogenously. [In layman's terms an anxious depressive, probably due to internal causes, but later via external issues.]

Heredity ratios: The mother was treated at the neurological-psychiatric ward, Bulovka hospital for melancholy.

Social conditions: The wife is in England. He was interned from 3.11.43 to 3.5.44.

The patient's father states: After coming home from prison (May 1944) he suffers from insomnia and great fear, he does not state why, he constantly wants to wash his hands in water. He is very nervous, when you talk to him, he doesn't jump up. He does nothing at home and sits or lies down.

Illnesses: Depression, fear and anxiety in the whole body. I think it is caused by the fact that he was in Terezín prison. At home he had the impression that his head was so heavy he would not get stronger. He needs something to calm him down so he could sleep. Lately everything has been 'pissing him off'. His mood is pretty sad. Sometimes he is tired of life, he has the impression that he is being controlled by a guard, which bothers him the most.

Physical findings: Finger and eyelid tremor. Otherwise, the neurological level is normal.

Prescribed: Sedatives.

Dr Hofmeister.

Augustin Preucil and his family – especially his mother, were suffering with their nerves and anxiety. The family knew their son 'Gustav' had been a Gestapo agent and justice and vengeance would be swift, once the authorities tracked him down.

Once he was arrested and under investigation, the Extraordinary People's Court in Prague was concerned enough about the psychiatric condition of Augustin Preucil, to permit another mental health assessment. This report (page 426 in the court case file) states:

> **Medical request for examination of Preucil's mental state:**
>
> Legal representative Koci a lawyer in Prague, filed a complaint to have the mental state of the detained Augustin Preucil examined.
>
> The current legal representative Jaroslav Mellan has found out that the mental state has not been examined yet and therefore asks that it be done and states that in February 1945, he was under medical treatment by Dr Hofmeister in the Bulovka hospital.
>
> His illness could already be observed from early childhood and worsened significantly when he suffered an injury in a crash in Benešov as a pilot of the Masaryk Aviation League in 1934. Marie Preucil suffers from permanent melancholy and is under constant medical care.
>
> After an examination, the medical staff confirmed the previous diagnosis and confirmed his mother's condition.

The claim of a crash and a head injury in 1934 is odd, as according to records and Preucil's own interview notes, he only learned to fly in 1935. The only head injury he ever mentioned was that sustained during the forced landing in Belgium in September 1941. Was this another fabrication he had fed to the doctors in a bid to save himself?

Also contained in the file was a notebook with notes in Preucil's handwriting. The papers contained a large number of German words and their Czech translations. These were the notes shown to Preucil in his interrogation. He claimed they were from his time in Terezín, where the prisoners were ordered to learn German.

Undoubtedly, there were many other documents that would have incriminated Preucil, if the Nazi regime had not been so meticulous in destroying their paperwork and evidence at the end of the war.

One document that did survive and incriminate Preucil from 1941, was the Gestapo report considering the financial reward for his arrival from England. A photograph of this can be seen within the photographic plates of this book with a translation.

It appears the report, dated 2 December 1941, reached the highest echelons of the Nazi regime, with adjutant and assistant to Hitler Julius Schaub, and General Bodenschatz, the liaison officer between Hitler and Hermann Göring, both featuring within the text.

What is also interesting, is the fact the report states the reward is to be 5,000 Reichsmarks and not the 10,000 Reichsmarks stated by the witnesses.

The investigation team were now finalising their case against Augustin Preucil and it did not look promising for the traitor.

Chapter Fourteen

Post war reports, Muriel and the Preucil family

One aspect of this story that cannot and should not be forgotten is Muriel, the 19-year-old wife of Augustin Preucil, left behind in Sunderland in September 1941.

Augustin and Muriel had been married for just seventy-nine days when he fled to Belgium. Posted missing – believed killed, Muriel received the dreaded telegram on 19 September 1941; although she was probably aware on the night he disappeared when he failed to come home. The dreaded telegram was followed in time, by the award of a war widow's pension.

Thankfully, Muriel did not know her husband was alive in Czechoslovakia and having a string of affairs with other women.

As his young wife started to rebuild her life, information started to filter through the intelligence networks about Preucil. As we have seen, the British intelligence services received information early on from the renowned 'Clarence' network in Belgium. Clarence reported Preucil's arrival and the betrayal of the local Belgian civilians. This information appears to have been passed on to the Inspectorate of the Czechoslovakian Air Force as early as 1 December 1941.

A few days later on the 9 December 1941, a secret message was sent by Brigadier General Karel Janousek of the Inspectorate to the Czech Ministry of National Defence (MNO) in London. Janousek, who headed the Czech fighter squadrons in Britain, had Major Jan Ambrus as one of his officers at the Inspectorate, while Major Karel Šifner was at the Ministry of National Defence in London. In his message General Janousek stated:

> Sergeant Preucil was a pilot in the year 1938 with the squadron Let. Pl. 4 in Prague. Recently, before his disappearance, he should have been brought before a court of law for air misconduct (low-flying). There is no news about this.
>
> Personality: Talkative, boastful, likes to explain/talk about himself. Likes to socialise with women, but was married and his English was poor.
>
> It is possible that he lost his way on his last flight and accidentally landed on the ground, since similar cases often happened to both English and German flights.
>
> However, it is also possible to assume that he fled on purpose out of fear of the court martial, although it is quite improbable that he could have strayed from the place where he carried out his crimes.

It is clear the British and Czechoslovakian authorities knew Preucil was probably alive and involved in some form of treachery, but further information was hard to come by. Muriel was told nothing.

In May 1942, I.G. Shreeve of the RAF Casualty Unit contacted Flight Lieutenant Sommerfield at the Prisoner of War section of the Air Ministry. He highlighted the fact that

Preucil had been reported missing on 18 September 1941, and the Czech air force had stated, that on 1 December 1941, they had received information from 'British Sources' to the effect that Sergeant Preucil was alive. (It appears the British intelligence services had not bothered to tell their own Royal Air Force directly, or it had been lost in communication.)

As no further information had been received from any source, I.G. Shreeve was asked if the PoW department had any other intelligence regarding Preucil. Unfortunately, no other information was available and MI9, who assisted with PoW intelligence, also had nothing.

Apart from the intelligence services, it appears the British authorities remained oblivious to the fact that not only was Preucil alive, but he was an active traitor. It is unclear, even in 2023, whether the British intelligence services (SIS) and/or the Special Operations Executive (SOE), had communicated any information back to Britain regarding Augustin Preucil. This is because there are no publicly available British records that comment on Preucil and his activities.

The Czech authorities, however, had long memories and it is clear they had probably received further intelligence about their man from their own sources. As we have seen, this resulted in an urgent order to arrest Augustin Preucil, Karel Čurda and Viliam Gerik as soon as the Nazi regime was deposed.

Preucil was arrested on 19 May 1945, within days of the resumption of Czech governance. Surprisingly, it appears the restored Czechoslovakian regime did not inform their British allies about his arrest, as there is nothing in the publicly available British files to this effect.

The restored Czech Ministry of National Defence in Prague were keen to prosecute the traitors and the court case file contains the following report to the Czech Ministry of National Defence, dated 22 August 1945 (on page 292.) Translated into English it states:

MNO

Subject Sergeant Augustin Preucil criminal proceedings.

In June 1945 in the criminal case of Sergeant Augustin Preucil:

I submit this report:

The accused is being prosecuted on suspicion of the crime of Defection according to s.183, 198 of the Criminal Code; Military Treason according to s.6c 1, 2 act c. 50/23 to which the decision Coll. Cooperation with the Gestapo.

The accused did not return on 18/9/1941 from a training flight, which he had undertaken from Sunderland airport in England. He made an emergency landing in Belgium and was transported to Prague. The Gestapo paid him 100,000Kr for bringing the plane.

After interrogation, he was released and the accused certainly maintained contact with the Gestapo. He is reasonably under suspicion that he cooperated in the interrogation of prisoner of war airmen, he also reported civilians to the Gestapo for their anti-German activities.

The field prosecutor, to whom the decision to release the accused from custody was submitted for comment, insists on custody due to the nature of the crimes. Since investigative procedure has not yet been completed, it is not possible to recommend release of the accused from custody.

Chief of the Field Court
Skpt. Justice JU. Dr Vohryzek František.

The lack of apparent communication between the Czechoslovakian government or the Czech Air Force and the British is surprising, especially as the British fought so hard to protect captured Czech airmen from the Nazi firing squads or guillotine between 1940 to 1945. Had they informed the British in some shape or form, or was there an element of embarrassment which prevented the flow of information?

In Britain, Muriel was oblivious to events in Prague and the fact her husband was alive and in custody as a traitor.

At some point in the summer of 1945, it appears the parents – or rather the father – of Preucil wrote to Muriel in Sunderland. At what point Preucil told his parents about his English wife and asked them to contact her is unknown, but it must have been an earth-shattering shock for Muriel when the letter dropped on the doormat. Not only did it announce her husband was alive and well, but he was in a cell in Prague's Pankrác Prison.

Unfortunately, this letter, or at least a copy of it, was not passed on to the Air Ministry in London or any other section of the authorities, so we cannot say what it actually stated. (Muriel's surviving family also do not possess any letters from the time.) It would appear Muriel wrote back to the Preucils, but again what was said is unknown.

Muriel, almost certainly confused by events, started to be sucked into the lies and fabrication of her husband. How many more letters passed between Muriel and his parents are unknown, but the Air Ministry file in the UK National Archives does contain copies of two further letters from Preucil's parents to Muriel. It also appears that Muriel tried to ascertain what was happening in Prague, but without much success.

A letter from Preucil's parents in Trebsin, dated 6 February 1946, stated:

Our Dear Muriel!

Please to accept our kindest love and best regards and hearty kisses by your Gustav and just the same from us his parents. Gustav thinks and remembers how you are getting on. Always when I call on him, his first question is about you and asks, if you are writing to us. The contents of your letter I tell him orally. He is still staying in prison of national court here in Prague – Pankrác.

You write that Ministry of Air, Red Cross and Embassy in Prague did not answer your application. Gustav asks you to urge it again, because he desires to get a definitive answer. And please let us know the result.

He wants also, if you could get a certificate by your Ministry, the he – Gustav – was in connection, spring of 1945 with English radio station 'Coctail' home station – Moravska Ostrava, Mr Vasut has it and it was brought by Mr Seignet.

We are sending to Gustav every fortnight clean linen, a parcel of 3kg food, cigarettes and we are permitted to visit him every 14 days. Please do everything possible to get Gustav out of prison, because he does not feel guilty.

Mother is seriously ill with her nerves, many hearty regards once more, and please to tell your parents our kindest love, we are sending contemporaneously with Gustav.

Yours sincere, please write soon!
Augustin Preucil (snr.)

This letter is not the first time, evidence has pointed to claims Augustin Preucil was working with the resistance or British SIS/SOE agents in his homeland towards the end of the war. I have spent many hours checking SIS and SOE reports to identify an English radio station called Coctail (or more likely Cocktail) in Moravska-Ostrava. SOE do not appear to have had any such radios or operations with this code name, but SIS have not released all their files. Despite this, a search of various volumes on the history of MI6 (SIS) during the Second World War and the years just after, fails to identify any such radio station or operation. Neither can I identify a Mr Vasut or a Mr Seignet. The letter appears to indicate that the radio transmitter (if that is what it was), was in the possession of a Mr Vasut, having been 'brought' (from Britain?) by Mr Seignet.

It is highly likely this was just another of Preucil's stories in the hope of avoiding trial and national condemnation, but could he have been so desperate to save himself, that he had actually worked with the underground and British agents in 1945?

Whether Muriel ever contacted the Air Ministry, Red Cross or the British Embassy in Prague regarding her husband before the autumn of 1946 is unknown. Certainly, a search of the register of correspondence for the British Embassy in Prague in the UK National Archives at Kew fails to locate anything in the name of Muriel, Augustin Preucil or his parents. There was also no correspondence in the Air Ministry file on her missing husband from Muriel, until the autumn of 1946.

In the autumn of 1946, the Czech investigators were completing their investigation and it was now clear that Preucil's case was one of high treason. It was deemed to be so serious that the Field Court of the Military judicial system passed the case to the Extraordinary People's Court in Prague.

Muriel soon received another letter from Preucil's parents, which was later passed on to the Air Ministry and was included in their file. This time, the translated letter was dated the 12 September 1946. Preucil's parents now started to inform Muriel of the threat to her husband's life:

Our Dear Muriel,

Accept heartfelt greetings and kind thoughts from your husband Gustav and from us, his parents. We inform you that your husband Augustin Preucil is keeping well.

On the critical day he lost his way in the fog over the sea and as he has run out of petrol, he landed in Belgium near Arleton. He was hidden there by partisans in the home of Lieutenant Francois Adam. He was then caught by the Germans and deported to Terezín. Now, after the restoration of the Republic, our Czechs have arrested him as an English agent. He is in prison of the People's Court at Pankrác in Prague. He is unable to write to you.

Dear Muriel, we beg you to use your influence with the British Government and to intervene through the British Embassy in Prague that criminal proceedings against your husband and our son, Augustin Preucil, be stopped and he be released from prison.

During the war the Germans evicted us from our home, all our buildings were destroyed and everything ruined. Now the Ministry of Social Welfare has given us a little wooden house on loan, so as to enable us to return to our estate. We very much felt with you in your sorrow all that time when you did not know about the whereabouts of your Gustav. Since our son had left home, we have felt distressed with his fate and mother has got a nervous breakdown.

Do not come to us in Bohemia for the time being. As soon as Gustav will return home, we will join you in England. We beg you to write to us immediately on receipt of this letter.

Many fond regards to you and to your parents.

Your husband Gustav and his parents,
Augustin and Marie Preucil.

This letter to Muriel was very misleading and deceptive. Which elements were down to their son's deceptive words and which were due to their own misleading comments is unknown. Certain elements within the letter were clearly misleading and must have been apparent to the author when it was written.

Obviously Preucil's parents knew their son had arrived home in September 1941. He stayed with them, until sent to Terezín in 1943. Why would they state he had been sent to Terezín in 1941? There was also no mention of the money the Gestapo had given him, that the Gestapo had regular dealings with him, nor that they knew of at least one girlfriend in Czechoslovakia!

Why did they declare the Czechs had accused Augustin of being an English agent? Was this just confusion with the fact he was an alleged Gestapo agent? Taken together with the previous comments in the earlier letter, about working with the English radio station 'Coctail' (Cocktail), was their son just spinning a web of lies and deceit?

Preucil's parents must have been desperate to save their son and it would appear they were happy to mislead his young wife in a bid to protect their son's life and possibly obtain British political or military assistance.

What Muriel and her family in Sunderland must have been thinking is unimaginable. However, it would appear that upon receipt of this latest letter, she contacted the British Red Cross.

What she told them is not known, but they wrote to the Air Ministry on 22 October 1946 and the letter was passed to a Mr E. Cowan in the Casualty Bureau S.7. The Red Cross letter stated:

> Dear Sirs,
>
> Re: Sergeant Pilot Augustin Preucil 787344, Stationed at Usworth, Co. Durham:
>
> You informed us on October 22nd 1941 that the above-named Czech airman was reported missing on the 18th of September 1941. His wife, Mrs Preucilova, has now received a letter from her parents-in-law (copy of which we enclose), telling her that he is alive, but is being held as a British agent.
>
> Mrs Preucilova* is naturally desperately anxious to do anything possible to help her husband, and we would be most grateful if you would kindly get in touch with her. [They then provided her address in Sunderland.]
>
> Yours faithfully,
> **S.J. Warner.**
> [*Author: this is the correct Czech grammar for Mrs Preucil.]

The Red Cross letter apparently kick-started a number of urgent memos between the Casualty Bureau, the Pension Department and the Prisoner of War section in London.

On 23 October 1946, Mr E. Cowan from S.7 Casualty Bureau sent a minute to Squadron Leader Long at A.1.3(a)1 (PoW section).

The minute outlined the fact that Preucil had gone missing on 18 September 1941. It also mentioned that the Czech Air Force Inspectorate had informed the Casualty Bureau on 15 May 1942, that they had received information from 'British Sources' that the airman was alive, but they had received no further information since that time.

It also added that MI9 had been consulted in June 1943, but they too stated they had no information concerning the airman and had no confirmation of his survival forthcoming from any source.

Mr Cowan told Squadron Leader Long that the matter had been referred to him in the first instance for any comments, before being submitted to the PoW department of the War Office, for action with the appropriate authorities for the release of the airman.

At this juncture it is clear that the British authorities were still oblivious of the fact that a Czech pilot belonging to the wartime RAF Volunteer Reserve was being held as an enemy agent.

Squadron Leader Long of A.1.3(a), added that he had no comment to make on the matter of Sergeant Preucil RAFVR, and the file was sent to the PoW department for further investigation.

In November 1946, Muriel wrote to the Czech Consulate in London. As a consequence, they contacted the Ministry of Social Welfare in Prague on 21 November 1946. The report, which I have translated, is contained within the Czech court case file p.508, it states:

It is noted by the Ministry of National Defence (MNO) in London, ref: cj. 15959-VI/2 department 1941, that as of the 16 December 1941, Flight Sergeant Augustin Preucil was declared missing, and his wife was assessed and granted a widow's pension of £12-0-0 per month.

The debt owed by the Ministry of Pensions office allowance is £4-11-3 per month. On the basis of the regulation on the reduction of the widow's pension, the payment of the allowance was stopped as of the 31.3.1946. The appointee now receives an allowance of £1-3-4 per week from the British Ministry of Pensions.

After receiving the mentioned letter, the Consulate General asked the Ministry of Pensions about the suspension of Preucil's widow's pension and asked the local Ministry to kindly investigate the case and approve the procedure of the local office.

Consul General V. Razga.

The Czechoslovakian authorities, knowing that Augustin Preucil was alive and a suspected traitor, had suspended the war widow's pension received by Muriel.

In London, the Air Ministry sent an urgent message to their air attaché at the British Embassy in Prague, asking for enquiries to be made with the Czechoslovakian authorities.

On 20 December 1947, a secret cypher from the British Embassy was received by Mr E. Cowan at S.7 Casualty Bureau. It stated:

> I am still awaiting reply to official enquiry addressed to Czechoslovak General Staff citation 0103/7342.
>
> Understand unofficially however, that Preucil is held in Pankrác Prison, a reported employee of the Gestapo who used to act as interpreter and denouncer of Czechoslovak prisoners during the war. Will telegraph confirmation when received from General Staff.

On 16 January 1947, Cowan wrote to Muriel. In his letter he told her:

> I am directed to refer to the Department's letter of the 12 November 1946 [which is not in either the UK or Czech files], and previous communications concerning your husband 787344 Sergeant Augustin Preucil, Royal Air Force; and to inform you that the Department has now received confirmation that your husband is alive and is held in custody at Prague by the Czechoslovakian authorities.
>
> I am madam, your obedient servant,
> E. Cowan.

Mr Cowan had clearly decided not to inform Muriel of the unofficial allegations against her husband.

The contents of the file held in the UK National Archives indicate there was a series of other letters between Preucil's parents and Muriel. Sadly, these are no longer available and copies are not held in the British or Czech archive files.

On the 4 February 1947, Cowan received another letter from Muriel. It also had attached a letter from Preucil's father, but this one is not in the British file and its contents are unknown. Muriel forwarded it to Cowan, stating that she hoped it would help with their investigations and asking that it be returned to her as soon as possible. I expect it was returned, but her surviving family in 2023 have no knowledge of any of this and the letter is no longer available.

The Czech authorities appear to have been continually unreceptive to any liaison with the British over the issue of Augustin Preucil. Despite this, the Air Ministry continued to make enquiries via their air attaché in Prague – Group Captain G.M. Wyatt.

On the 8 February 1947, a report was received from Brigadier General J. Hanus. (Believed to be Josef Jan Hanus, a former RAF Volunteer Reserve pilot who had followed the same route to England via Poland and France. He served with No. 6 OTU and then 310 Squadron in 1940, so he had probably known Preucil personally.) His report stated:

Sgt. Gustav PREUCIL – Investigation.

The Ministry of National Defence, Headquarters Air Force Command, begs to inform you that criminal proceedings are being taken against Sergeant

PREUCIL A., who is suspected of the offences of military treason and denunciation, in that, after his desertion from England to Belgium on 18.9.1941 he handed over the English plane in return for a reward of 100,000 kr. and entered the service of the Gestapo, to whom he betrayed important facts.

After his landing he betrayed the civilians who provided him with civilian clothes and hid him, to the Gestapo. He collaborated with the Gestapo even after his return to Prague, and during the time in prison at Terezín, several persons who were either interned or condemned as a result of his denunciations lost their lives.

The case is at present in the process of investigation and will last a considerable time yet.

Brig. Gen. J. Hanus.

The report was translated and sent to the Director of Prisoners of War at the War Office in London by Group Captain Wyatt. The British must have now realised that Preucil, a man married to a British woman, was about to go on trial for his life. The covering letter from Group Captain Wyatt dated 21 February 1941 stated:

747344 Sergeant A. Preucil RAF (Czech):

With reference to your letter dated 3rd February 1947, you will see from the attached copy of a letter received from the Czechoslovak General Staff that the Czechs do not appear too willing to say all they know about the Preucil affair.

It is possible to force the issue and demand the handing over of Preucil, even temporarily, on the grounds that he deserted and betrayed British secrets to the enemy at a time when he was, presumably, subject to the Air Force Act. This is a point however, on which the Legal Departments of the War Office and Air Ministry could advise.

In the meantime, I will continue to press the General Staff for more details of the case.

G.W. Wyatt
Group Captain, Air Attaché, Prague.

While the British authorities sought to get to the bottom of the issue, Muriel was having her own problems with the cost of just day-to-day living.

On the 5 March 1947, she wrote to Mr Cowan again. She informed him that two weeks previously, she had been asked by the Ministry of Pensions (UK) to return her pension book to them. Muriel sent the book to the Ministry and was now suffering great hardship, as she only had £2-6-0d a week on which to survive. She asked if she was to be paid the allowances owed to her, as she, 'Could not go on without some financial help.'

She then asked if there was any news about her husband and what the charges were against him.

In reply on 13 March 1947, a Mr A.W. Livingston wrote to Muriel in Sunderland. His letter appears somewhat dismissive and uncaring:

Madam,

I am directed to refer to your letters of 15th January and 12th February 1947, regarding your husband Sergeant A. Preucil, and to say that information received from the Czechoslovakian authorities, indicates that he is held by them in the Pankrác Prison as a reported employee of the German Gestapo and a war collaborationist.

I am further to add that your husband, together with all Czechoslovakian personnel, were discharged from the Royal Air Force Volunteer Reserve with effect from 30th June 1946, further enquiries about him, is without the jurisdiction of this department. It is suggested therefore, that if you require any further information you should write to the Czechoslovak Ministry of National Defence in Prague.

Your letter of 6th February 1946 is returned forthwith [apparently this is the letter she asked to have returned the previous month].

A.W. Livingston.

Mr Livingston did not appear to have received Muriel's letter concerning her lack of finances and her pension when he wrote the letter, but once he had it in his possession, he wrote to her again on 19 March 1947. He told her that this had been referred to the appropriate Air Ministry branch who would write to her shortly. Whether she ever received a letter from them is unknown, but it appears her widow's pension was stopped.

What Muriel and the British authorities did not know, was that Preucil was about to go on trial at the Extraordinary People's Court in Prague within days. An indictment had been served upon him on 3 March 1947.

The first news arrived in Britain via the *Evening News* on 15 April 1947. Their newspaper headline stated: 'Spy in RAF shot his pupil, stole plane over Britain, Instructor to die for treason.'

The story, via the Reuters news agency, claimed that Preucil had shot his Polish pupil pilot before escaping to Belgium, where he had betrayed the Belgian civilians. Preucil then entered the service of the Gestapo and worked as a stool-pigeon in Terezín concentration camp. Now he had been sentenced to death.

The following day *The Times* had a similar headline: 'End of a Czech Informer, Traitorous career with Gestapo.'

This news must have been a hammer-blow to Muriel and her family, even though she would likely have expected it when the alleged charges were considered. The British authorities must have also been shocked by the sudden news.

The Czech court case file contains the following notice from April 1947 (it has been translated):

Defendant Augustine Preucil born 3 July 1914 in Trebsin.

He is guilty from 1939–1945 in the period of increased threat to the republic in Prague. From Poland and elsewhere.

1. He supported the Nazi movement by sending him to Poland as a Gestapo agent in 1939, where he joined the Czechoslovak army. He enlisted in the air force and after escaping from England by plane, he continued to be a Gestapo agent in Prague.
2. At the time mentioned above, i.e. during the war, he committed military treason by a.) he caused damage to the defence of the republic and its English ally by destroying an airplane [*sic*], and in England he shot at a Polish comrade who accompanied him. b.) In retaliation for voluntarily reporting to the German authorities, he revealed to them, i.e. to foreign powers, the facts, measures and objects that should have remained secret for the defence of the republic, whereby this crime was committed out of ignorance.
3. Sentenced to death.

The British authorities appear to have been taken completely by surprise and an urgent message was sent to Prague to confirm this. The new air attaché in Prague – Group Captain Cameron – contacted the Ministry of National Defence General Staff. The Czechoslovak authorities did not respond with great speed, but eventually replied in late May 1947, some five to six weeks after the verdict and execution.

After translating the letter from the Czech General Staff, Group Captain Cameron sent it to Cowan and the Assistant Chief of the Air Staff (Intelligence) on 30 May 1947. His attached note stated that he had received the reply from the Czechs in response to his, 'Frequent queries regarding the fate of Sgt. Preucil.'

After outlining the background to the case, the final paragraph of the Czech response stated: 'Augustin Preucil was sentenced to death by hanging by an Extraordinary People's Court in Prague on 14.4.1947.' The sentence was carried out the same day. In the carrying out of the sentence the demands of justice against a deserter and traitor to the British and Czechoslovak air forces were satisfied.

The Czech General Staff's letter was unsigned, abrupt and to the point. It was almost as if the issue was now closed and should be forgotten.

Even the Czech Consul General in London appeared to be taken by surprise. On 16 May 1947, an urgent message was sent to the Regional Criminal Court in Prague. The Consul in London stated that he had been contacted by Muriel Preucil asking for an official copy of the judgement, so she could see on what basis her husband had been sentenced to death.

What we now know is that he was tried by Chief Public Prosecutor Jaroslav Drabek. As usual in Czechoslovakia, after being found guilty and sentenced to death, he was executed the same day; but for some reason his execution was delayed until the evening.

Preucil was hanged using the traditional 'pole-hanging' method in the yard of Pankrác Prison. This form of execution was very different to the British long-drop method.

The day after his execution, the court issued a notice (contained within the court case file p.691) it stated:

RELEASE OF BODY FOR BURIAL

Confirmed

The court confirms the corpse of Augustin Preucil, convicted on April 14th 1947 and executed on the same day, was handed over to his father Augustin Preucil from Trebsin for a private burial.

The funeral will be carried out in the early hours of the morning, or late in the afternoon, with the participation of no more than 10 people from the closest relatives without any pomp and show.

April 15, 1947.

For copy and issue to father.

Muriel was not present for her husband's funeral ... and there is no record of where he was buried.

Muriel later became a schoolteacher, but had to stop working when she contracted tuberculosis which impacted her health and ability to teach.

Although Muriel was drawing a war widow's pension and living in the family home in Sunderland, her world had suddenly changed when she received the letters from the parents of

Preucil in Trebsin. In addition, the British authorities would soon stop her widow's pension when they became aware of Preucil's treachery. It was never reinstated.

Muriel remarried post-war and had a happy family, living until 2006 with her husband and children. (I have not named the family for reasons of privacy or where they lived, but I am very grateful to her children for speaking to me.)

Two weeks later, Karel Čurda and Viliam Gerik followed Preucil to the gallows at 11.45 hours on 29 April 1947. The two Special Operations Executive traitors were executed within twelve minutes of each other, bringing a sudden and swift end to the three men the Czech authorities had sought so urgently in May 1945.

Many people in Czechoslovakia or the modern-day Czech Republic have little time for Augustin Preucil or Karel Čurda. Both men were responsible for the deaths of a high number of patriotic Czechoslovakians between 1941 and 1945.

There are a number who feel that Viliam Gerik was a victim of circumstance. He was stranded in Czechoslovakia with little option but to turn himself in. The extent of his own treacherous actions is debatable, especially after the Gestapo imprisoned him in Terezín and Dachau, but he was ultimately betrayed by Augustin Preucil. The question is why did Preucil betray him? Was it to protect himself and his nefarious activities, or was it because he wanted to start a relationship with Milena Tomanova? Whatever the reasoning, Gerik was sold out by Preucil.

Whatever people believe, the fact is that these three men were the main (living) Czech traitors at the end of the war, (the likes of Grabovsky and Kindl were already dead).

Although Preucil is now dead, there were many questions that will probably never be answered. The main one is whether Preucil was, as he regularly claimed, a double agent? Even if he was, who was he working for – SOE, SIS, or even the Czechs?

In addition, who was his Gestapo, or Abwehr, contact while he was in Britain? Or was he not working for the Germans at that time?

As we have seen, Augustin Preucil told a number of people he was a British intelligence agent and he was quick to make this declaration in his first post-war interrogation. He also claimed to have been selected by his wife's brother-in-law and trained by the British security services – but can we corroborate such apparently fanciful claims?

The first issue is that we cannot identify his wife's brother-in-law. I have spoken with Muriel's son, and over time the family has become estranged and distanced. He cannot assist with names, let alone addresses eighty years later. I have also tried to identify siblings for Muriel without success via well-known heritage websites and records. I also made enquiries with the security services without success, but that is probably not surprising, especially if Muriel's brother-in-law was an intelligence officer.

In the next two chapters we will look at these unanswered questions in more detail.

Chapter Fifteen

Who was Preucil's contact in the United Kingdom?

As we have seen, there are a number of questions in the case of Augustin Preucil that were not answered – or even asked in the post-war Czech investigation.

The main issue is whether Augustin Preucil was still operating as an enemy agent in the United Kingdom and if he was, who was his contact and how did he receive and send messages? In addition, if he was no longer an active agent, why did he abscond with the Hurricane in September 1941?

As already stated, there are no other 'open' files in the UK National Archives in relation to Preucil and his activities as a German agent. A search of the archives also finds no trace of any 'closed' files. It is possible the Special Intelligence Service (SIS) still hold files on this subject, but to date, they have not been made available for public scrutiny and my enquiries have received no response.

There appears to be no doubt that Preucil was an active agent in Poland, and it would seem from Josef Chalupský's evidence that he was also sending messages from Chartres near Paris in 1939–40. Whether the messages from either Poland or France were of any benefit to the Gestapo, and by association the Luftwaffe, is debatable. We have no detailed evidence of what was sent to the Gestapo and Preucil naturally claims the messages were of no intelligence value.

The speed with which France and the Low-Countries collapsed was a surprise to everyone and probably went beyond the wildest dreams of the German intelligence services in 1940. If Preucil, as suspected, was still an active agent in France, his sudden evacuation and departure to Gibraltar and then England, would have caused a severe headache for the Gestapo. How could they possibly keep track of him and maintain contact, when even he did not know where he was going from one day to the next?

When he arrived in England in July 1940, Preucil was dispatched to the Czech Depot at RAF Cosford in the West Midlands. Within weeks he was at RAF Sutton Bridge on the Lincolnshire-Norfolk border and in October and November, he was at RAF Usworth just outside Sunderland. Over the next few months, he was posted a number of times to Scotland, the West Country, possibly Northern Ireland and then back to Usworth again. It was so hard to keep track of him, it appears even the RAF personnel records unit had problems keeping up with him. So how could the Gestapo possibly locate and communicate with their man?

In 1940 and 1941, the RAF and the British intelligence services were concerned that some of the new Czech (and Polish) arrivals, may be communists and German sympathisers. To counter this, they spent a great deal of time checking and interviewing the arriving airmen, but some, like Preucil, may have slipped through the net. Was there another enemy agent in the air force communicating with Preucil?

With the regular and systematic questioning of Czech airmen, the fact that Preucil was keen to tell his Czech interrogators he felt under suspicion in England is no surprise. If he felt ostracised by not being sent to a dedicated Czechoslovakian fighter squadron like 310 or 312 squadrons, he may have felt under suspicion. However, from the evidence of other airmen contained within this book and the Czech court records, it is clear he was considered to be undisciplined, lazy, a womanising gambler and a poor team member – hardly the qualifications for a hand-picked Czechoslovakian-manned squadron!

Some people over the years have said Preucil was ordered to fly a new cannon-armed Hawker Hurricane to the Germans so they could examine it. But this needs closer examination.

The Hawker Hurricane was the backbone of the RAF during the Battle of France, the withdrawal from Dunkirk and the Battle of Britain. Armed with eight .303 Browning machine guns like its contemporary the Supermarine Spitfire, pilots wanted a cannon-armed fighter like their opponent – the Messerschmitt 109E. While the Spitfire developed into the cannon-armed Spitfire Mk.V, the Hurricane Mk.II was also developed with a cannon armament.

In early 1941, the new Hurricanes were starting to reach front-line squadrons on the Channel coast, but Preucil's own unit – 55 Operation Training Unit at Usworth – was still operating the Hurricane Mk.I, many of which had long operational histories throughout the spring and summer of 1940.

It has been claimed by some that Preucil served for a time with 605 Squadron. They were receiving the cannon-armed

Hurricane Mk.II in 1941 and this may be where the story of a German directive originates.

There is a problem with this claim, however. According to the 605 Squadron Operational Record Book (ORB) in the UK National Archives, there is no mention of Preucil ever joining or flying with the unit. In addition, his RAF personal record does not list an attachment to 605 Squadron. Therefore, this claim appears to be totally incorrect, and a myth.

Despite being able to discount this allegation against Preucil, there is documented evidence in the UK National Archives that another pilot from occupied France was recruited with the specific aim of joining the RAF and stealing an aircraft and flying it back to the Nazis (Jean Fraval, reference KV2/2246).

The fact that Josef Chalupský and others in the Gestapo were allegedly excited that Preucil had brought a 'new type of aircraft' over to Belgium is also misleading. Any student of Nazi psychology will know that Hitler's minions did not want to give him any bad news, only the good news. The same could be said all the way down the Nazi rank structure, as failure was not an option.

The theft of a new 'secret' Hurricane and its delivery to Preucil's Nazi masters is therefore a myth. Although he arrived with an older Mk.I Hurricane, his Gestapo masters and perhaps even the Luftwaffe, were only too happy to tell the Higher Command that they had a new type of British fighter delivered to them by their 'top agent'.

The news of Preucil's arrival with the Hurricane clearly reached the highest echelons of the Nazi regime. The reward memorandum (see photographic plates) from Berlin clearly names the Reichsführer (Himmler), Gruppenführer Schaub (adjutant to Hitler) and General Bodenschatz (the liaison officer between Hitler and Göring) within its text, and them being aware of Preucil's defection.

To return to Preucil's time in the United Kingdom, it is likely that any letters and communications by Czechoslovakian (and Polish) airmen were thoroughly checked by the censors. Therefore, the likelihood of him writing and receiving written communications and instructions like those he sent from Poland and France is very low.

One possibility is that he sent information via the postal network to a neutral country. Posting a letter well away from his airfield and using a code name or another alias known to the Gestapo was an option, but not infallible. Lisbon in neutral Portugal was a favourite destination for such letters, but the censors and the post office, not to mention MI5 and Special Branch, were well aware of this route and would open and check letters.

As already mentioned, it is possible another Czech or Allied airman could have been an agent and acted as a conduit between the Gestapo and Preucil. The question is, who could this be and how could this work?

We know Preucil was with a number of Czechoslovakian and Polish pilots at Sutton Bridge, Usworth and other airfields. The problem is how could they maintain contact with him when he was moved around so often?

It is possible that his communication with his contact and/or the Gestapo was intermittent, with long periods of non-reporting because of his movements. (Josef Chalupský mentioned this in his interview and described the joy Oskar Fleischer displayed when it appeared Preucil had written to them from Paris in 1940. The Gestapo man had previously openly complained in front of Chalupský, 'The guy does not write'.) But what if the German and Gestapo intelligence services *were* able to keep pace with him, possibly passing him from one agent to another? There would need to have been a widespread network of agents, as too much travelling in wartime Britain could have led to suspicion.

To consider the feasibility of this we must briefly look at the make-up of the German intelligence services in 1940 and 1941.

The German military intelligence service, known as the Abwehr, was a well-structured and efficient system in 1939 to 1941. Staffed by military officers and headed by Admiral Wilhelm Canaris, it liaised with the senior command of all three military services including the Gestapo.

The Abwehr ran various operations and recruited agents for work in foreign nations including Britain. The man at the head of the organisation, Admiral Canaris, although initially a supporter of Hitler, started to doubt him and he was eventually arrested in 1944 and executed along with many other Abwehr officers.

In the early part of the war, Canaris and Reinhard Heydrich, who was head of SS intelligence at the time, had an amicable relationship. This relationship did not hide the fact that the Nazis still blamed the officer classes, and in particular the Abwehr, for failures during the First World War. Canaris knew the SD (SS intelligence – Sicherheitsdienst) monitored the Abwehr's telephones and even carried out surveillance of his staff.

The SD and the Gestapo not only gathered and held their own intelligence, but they now also recruited and deployed their own agents, men and women like Augustin Preucil.

Things reached a climax when Heydrich was posted to Czechoslovakia in September 1941, (coincidentally the same month Preucil disappeared). After a heated argument, Heydrich asked for the Abwehr to be placed under the control of the SD and Gestapo. This did not occur, but their previous cooperation started to falter.

In the early part of the war, the German intelligence services had little success in Britain and many agents were captured and turned. Many of the agents sent to Britain were not Germans but men and women from occupied Europe – many carrying out their work under Nazi duress. Suffice to say for this book, there was one turned agent called Wulf Schmidt, known to MI5 as 'Tate' and to the Abwehr as 'Leonhardt'. As we shall see, this might have had a bearing on Augustin Preucil.

Wulf Schmidt was Danish and sent to Britain by parachute in September 1940. Unfortunately for Schmidt, a previous agent had been captured and turned and he tipped off MI5 about Schmidt's imminent arrival. When he arrived, Schmidt was almost instantly detained. Fearing execution, Schmidt accepted the offer to work for MI5 as a double agent in October 1940.

Wulf Schmidt continued to send messages to the Abwehr, but they started to fear he may have been detained and smelt a possible rat. They therefore sent another agent, Karel Richter (often known as Karl Richter) to check all was well.

Richter was a Czech citizen like Preucil and came from the Sudetenland, the area with a high number of ethnic Germans.

Despite being sent to England, his language skills in both German and English were poor. Richter was parachuted into England in the early hours of the 12 May 1941. He landed at London Colney in Hertfordshire and immediately buried his flight suit, helmet and some food. He walked off with his radio transmitter and his service pistol.

According to the MI5 files held in the UK National Archives, Richter appears to have wandered around for two days before being detained by a police constable on 14 May. The officer found Richter's fake ID card to be incorrect, while he was also in possession of a valid Czechoslovakian passport.

When MI5 interrogated Richter at Latchmere House (Camp 020), he told them he had been a seaman on cross Atlantic ships, but that when the war started his ship was held in Hamburg and so he decided to escape to Sweden. He managed to cross the Baltic Sea, but was detained by the Swedes for not having the correct visa and returned to Germany. Upon his return the Gestapo arrested him and sent him to the Fuhlsbuttel concentration camp.

In a near repeat of the tactics allegedly used on Preucil, who had also been trying to leave the country, Richter claimed he was offered a way out by the Gestapo. He could gain his freedom in return for some dangerous work for them, otherwise he would be returned to the concentration camp.

Unsurprisingly, Richter accepted and signed an agreement or protocol (similar to that the Czech authorities now held for Preucil). It stated he would work faithfully for the Reich and Adolf Hitler; if he failed, action would be taken against his family in Czechoslovakia.

Richter claimed he was trained in Hamburg by a Dr Bruhns (identified by MI5 as Hauptmann Bruhns, but also known as Beyer.) He told his interrogators he was trained with two other agents, concentrating on various types of British aircraft, anti-aircraft guns and barrage balloon defences. He was taught to use a wireless transmitter and codes, but he claimed his Morse skills were poor and Dr Bruhns decided he was not suitable for a deployment to Britain.

Richter then claimed to have been approached by a Dr Scholz, who knew Dr Bruhns. Scholz told him he had a role for him, which did not need Morse skills and that he would be with another agent who was more proficient and experienced – in fact Scholz called him 'our best man'.

In January 1941, Richter claimed he was taken to Amsterdam in a bid to get a fishing boat to convey him to England, but nothing suitable could be found. Taken back to Hamburg, he was shown how to use a new type of radio transmitter.

Eventually, he was ready to go again (on 9 May 1941) and was taken by motor launch to be landed on the English coast at an unknown location. This landing, Richter claimed, was prevented by a heavy sea swell and they returned once more to The Netherlands.

In the early hours of the 12 May, Richter was taken by a twin engine aircraft from Schiphol airport and ordered to parachute from 30,000ft using a static line. He claimed he had to use oxygen for the flight, but baled-out without it, almost losing consciousness on the way down. He later claimed to have been ill for a short time after landing, possibly due to his descent without oxygen.

Who was Preucil's contact in the United Kingdom?

Richter landed in London Colney, Hertfordshire, and hid his parachute and flying overalls as well as some food. He then took his radio transmitter and pistol before leaving the immediate area of his landing.

Richter told the MI5 interrogators that his role was to meet with an unnamed man at the Regent Palace Hotel in London and check that he was still an active agent. He had in his possession, a large amount of cash, totalling over £551 and $1,400, and a radio crystal which was to be handed to an agent.

The unnamed agent was, as far as MI5 were concerned, the turned agent 'Tate' and they knew everything about Richter's arrival and the planned meeting in London (Tate having received the radio instructions from the Germans). They believed the radio crystal was probably for Tate and also the money.

Once content that the agent was still active and loyal to the Germans, Richter was to collect information about the roads and railways, their condition and whether they were defended. He was also to check if identification was needed to stay in a hotel and whether gas masks were usually carried. The checks on roads reflected the directions Preucil had mentioned in his debriefing in 1941.

Why Karel Richter wandered around the area of his landing for two days and had not moved on is unclear, but it appears MI5 were not unduly concerned by this. (Most agents and aircrew who had baled-out would ordinarily vacate their landing place as soon as possible to avoid detection.) Was Richter waiting to meet another contact who failed to arrive at London Colney?

There has been speculation over the years that Richter was to observe the de Havilland factory near his landing place.

de Havilland was developing the Mosquito fighter-bomber, but by this time, the aircraft was being test flown at Boscombe Down in Wiltshire, not Hertfordshire.

Richter initially told MI5 he had arrived by boat at Cromer in Norfolk (possibly the location he should have been dropped by the fishing boat). Then he started to use the regular evasion tactic of claiming he just wanted to escape the Nazis. He gave the address of a Jewish woman in London whom he had met in Germany before the war, claiming he had handled her finances (this was later confirmed by a Special Branch visit to the woman). Richter said he wanted to meet her again and go to the United States, the large amount of money was for his transport. He also claimed he had wanted to go to the Czech Consul, although he could never explain why he had not done so.

Later, Richter changed his account and stated that the radio transmitter had not been for the other unnamed agent in London. He claimed the radio was for his own emergency use, but he had no codes and he should have had no need to use the transmitter before leaving the country. MI5 did not believe this account and wondered why he would carry such a heavy and incriminating device around if it was only for an emergency?

Tests on the radio transmitter Richter possessed by the MI5 technical team, found it to be a new very efficient system and much more powerful than previous captured sets they had examined.

News of Richter's capture was withheld from the media, as MI5 did not want to let the enemy to know he had been captured and, by extension, the possibility Wulf Schmidt (Tate) had been turned.

Richter was tried at the Old Bailey in camera (in secret), found guilty and sentenced to death. He appealed against the verdict, stating he had been forced to come to England and that the jury did not believe the account that he was to meet the man in London. He added that he had done nothing to harm England and had even offered to fight against the Nazis.

In the MI5 files at the UK National Archives (reference KV2/31), there is a report dated the 15 July 1941, which states that it was believed the radio transmitter and spare parts were for the agent 'Tate', or an unidentified third person.

However, during practical tests and further interrogation, Richter showed he could build a radio transmitter and more. On 21 August 1941, Ronald Thomas Reed, an intelligence radio specialist, sent a report to Major Thomas Argyll Robertson of MI5.

Robertson was known as TAR and was responsible for disinformation and the double cross network of agents. Ronald Thomas Reed was a radio specialist who had worked with the BBC and worked on the double agent network and disinformation including Operation Mincemeat, the disinformation about Allied landings in the Mediterranean in 1943. In fact, the corpse used to disseminate the fake invasion plans to the Nazis had a fake ID card bearing Reed's own photographic image.

Reed's report stated that, in his opinion, the earlier assessment of Richter's technical knowledge and ability should be considerably revised as a result of seeing the transmitter he had built, and having heard him send Morse messages. Richter had also explained to Reed how he would test a radio transmitter. In summary, Richter was not the novice and poor Morse man he claimed to be.

It is clear from the MI5 files that Richter was actually a very proficient radio expert who had been in possession of a new, powerful and efficient type of transmitter. He may well have been sent to check on 'Tate's' loyalty to the fatherland, but he appears to possibly have had other orders.

On 29 November 1941, Richter was in Wandsworth Prison awaiting his appointment with the nation's hangman, Albert Pierrepoint. In one final meeting with an MI5 officer, he changed his account again and admitted the transmitter was for his own use and no other person.

On the 5 December 1941, Colonel William Edward Hinckley-Cooke of MI5, decided that Richter could be of no further assistance to them. Hinckley-Cooke reported that Richter had made rambling statements, making it impossible to believe anything he said. 'His explanation that the odd radio crystal he had in his possession was for 'Tate' with a different aerial, was uncertain and how this could be technically possible was unclear.'

In essence, the file was being closed on Richter and he was hanged in Wandsworth Prison on 10 December 1941. Richter did not go quietly like other executed spies. He struggled violently with his executioners, headbutting the wall and breaking his restraining straps. A process which normally took less than ten to fifteen seconds to complete, took over seventeen minutes.

It is clear MI5 never understood why Karel Richter had wandered around the area of the drop zone for two days, instead of heading as planned to London to meet with 'Tate'. They had also been unable to ascertain who the new radio transmitter was actually for and there was the issue of a lack of codes and the odd radio crystal.

Richter's radio skills were clearly well above those of a man who said he was held back from operations due to his poor Morse skills.

The situation becomes even stranger when we consider the following: on 31 January 1941, another agent had arrived by parachute in Cambridgeshire. His name was Josef Jakobs, a German citizen who had been born in Luxembourg.

Jakobs was a member of the Luftwaffe sent to England to send back weather reports to assist Luftwaffe bombings raids. Unfortunately, when he landed he broke his ankle and was detained almost immediately along with his radio transmitter and a pistol, which he used to summon assistance by firing it into the air.

Held in custody by MI5 and interrogated, Jakobs was informed a few months later of the arrival of Richter. The two men were placed in the same room to be covertly observed and recorded via hidden microphones on 1 July 1941.

Later, believing the British knew all about Richter, Jakobs told his interrogators that they had trained together and the Czech was a wireless expert who trained others in radio transmitter construction. If true, this corroborated Reed's technical assessment and Richter was certainly not the novice he claimed to be.

This assistance did not save Jakobs and he was shot a few weeks later, on 15 August 1941, at the Tower of London.

After Richter was executed, MI5 continued their enquiries and Reed submitted another report in January 1942. He had conducted a further technical assessment of the radio equipment seized from Richter in May 1941 and found the odd radio crystal to be too powerful for 'Tate's' radio transmitter and Richter's. He therefore concluded that this crystal was either for an unidentified third party and another radio transmitter, or those who supplied Richter with his equipment had made a mistake.

On reflection, there is no doubt that Richter, a Czech with a poor command of the English and German languages, had been sent to meet and check on the agent Wulf Schmidt (Tate). But was there more to his arrival?

There are unanswered questions about Richter to this day. What his plans were after contacting 'Tate' is unclear, although he did mention some spurious instructions about roads, railways, hotels and gas masks. He said he was to head for the coast and get a boat back to the Continent, but MI5 believed these alleged instructions were not very detailed and appeared to be false.

Why did Richter wander around in Hertfordshire for two days when he was supposed to be heading into London to meet 'Tate'?

Why did he claim to be poor at Morse, then display a high level of technical knowledge and practical skills to MI5? Why was this not pursued by MI5? (Could Richter have decided to give increasing amounts of information about his abilities to MI5, in the hope he could postpone a trial and execution?)

Josef Jakobs told MI5 that Richter was an expert in transmitters who trained others.

The radio was a new, powerful and efficient system according to technical reports. But where was his code book?

Even before his execution, MI5 believed there could be another unidentified agent, but this does not seem to have been pursued.

In summary, we appear to have had a Czech national under similar threats as Preucil in England. He was apparently a radio expert who trained others and had a spare radio crystal and a new, more powerful and efficient radio transmitter.

Initially, Richter claimed the radio was for 'Tate' and then for himself, although it was just for emergencies. Could it be that the radio and the training which this Czech expert could provide, was actually for our Czechoslovakian pilot Augustin Preucil? Or was there another go-between?

On 12 May 1941, the day Richter arrived in England, Preucil was attached to RAF Kemble in Gloucestershire, having only arrived there twenty-one days before from Hullavington in Wiltshire. The next day (13 May) he transferred back to Hullavington in Wiltshire, both airfields are about 100 miles from where Richter was captured. Is it possible there was a meeting planned, but Preucil or another party did not, or could not, attend? Was Preucil caught up in an unexpected transfer after just twenty-one days at Kemble and could not attend? We cannot say, as the RAF records do not show enough detail to consider this further.

We will probably never know whether there was a link between Richter and Preucil and this is pure speculation – but it might just be plausible. Although Richter's capture was kept secret until long after Preucil's flight to Belgium, is it possible that the fact an agent had failed to attend a meeting could have caused Preucil to panic and eventually flee?

The accounts of Preucil being court-martialled for low-flying cannot be found in RAF records, although that does not mean he was not about to be charged. Again, this may have been just speculation – or even if true, a handy deflection for Preucil's flight to Belgium. After all, he could hardly tell everyone in Britain, and later the Czech investigators, that he feared immediate arrest after a meeting with his Nazi contact had failed.

We have no surviving Gestapo and Luftwaffe records of his debriefings in Belgium, Berlin or Prague. If Preucil was to have met up with Karel Richter or another agent, those records may have shown this.

It is likely the full MI5 records concerning Preucil (if they exist), may never be opened to public scrutiny, but there is one final thing to consider. The British security services were having a great deal of success capturing and turning German agents, how could Preucil have managed to remain undercover while so many agents were being turned?

In the next section, we shall consider whether Preucil could actually have been trained and employed as a British double agent as he claimed so many times to his associates and to the Czech authorities.

Chapter Sixteen

Could Preucil have been a double agent?

Was Augustin Preucil a double agent and actually working for the British intelligence services?

On face value it seems implausible, especially as his 'trade-craft' was apparently so poor, and he told so many people he was a British or Czech agent. But what if he was under-trained and under so much pressure after four years in Czechoslovakia, that he cracked under the mental strain?

The question of whether Preucil was a British agent, is one that can be argued from both sides with some credibility.

If we start with the British intelligence services, would they really use a Czech sergeant with a poor discipline record? He had just married an English girl and was apparently happy to settle down in England. Conversely, we know he was a womanising gambler, who also drank and probably attracted too much attention to himself. These are hardly the vocational qualities of an agent.

We know British intelligence successfully turned a number of German spies during the war. If Preucil had told the British authorities that he was under the direction of the Gestapo and German intelligence services, could they have used him as a double agent?

If Richter had been sent to train and check on Preucil in May 1941, surely his capture would have been good cause for the Czech pilot to flee back to the Gestapo. We know Richter's arrest and trial were not reported until after Preucil had fled, but if a contact had not turned up for a meeting, he might have feared compromise and detection before deciding to flee. Conversely, this would also be a good cover story for a turned Gestapo agent to return home and work for the British – taking a Hurricane Mk.1 with him.

Preucil claimed to have told a number of Czechoslovakian officers and other officials about his Gestapo connection, but if this is true, it appears no one ever took any action. What is also surprising is that the post-war investigators do not appear to have followed up these lines of enquiry and spoken to any person named by Augustin Preucil. Why?

In modern British law, failure to do this would probably lead to an unsafe conviction and a retrial.

If the Czech officers and officials were not listening to Preucil in 1940 and 1941, did he then decide to tell the British? And if he did, what did they do?

Preucil claimed to have been approached by his wife's brother-in-law, and recruited into the British intelligence services. There is no documented evidence to support this, but neither is there any evidence in the Czech file or in Britain that anyone ever followed this up. (Although of course the SIS files, if there are any on this subject, are not in the public domain and available for inspection.)

There is undeniable historical evidence, SIS did not take kindly to the Special Operations Executive's work. SIS clearly believed SOE were nothing more than 'a bunch of amateurs treading on their expert toes'. But would they go out of their way to cause problems for SOE agents in 'the field'?

We know from the records, there were arguments over the resources used to drop agents and supplies into Europe, but could the SIS have recruited Preucil and sent him to see what the SOE agents were up to in Prague?

It is possible that Preucil could have been recruited by SIS and given some training, and what better way of delivering him back to the Nazis was there, than his own Hurricane to Belgium? (As we have seen, there is no evidence to corroborate the claims by some that Preucil was directed to take a cannon-armed Hurricane Mk.II back to the Germans. This was, in effect, old technology and not a great loss to the British – but it could be an excellent 'sweetener' for a returning agent.)

However, the allegations of a possible court martial for poor flying, while also being a good cover for him fleeing, could also be genuine, although cannot be confirmed.

The issue of him betraying Viliam Gerik to the Gestapo could be a case of an SIS agent dealing with a treacherous SOE man, but it is likely Preucil was more interested in the young lady – Milena Tomanova.

It is also likely that many of the things Preucil said about his training as an agent were actually learnt from his time speaking with the SOE traitors in Prague. He could use this information to spin his web of lies, while gaining the confidence of people he would later betray.

However, there is the issue in 1945–1947 of why the Czech authorities did not update the British with details of Preucil's arrest, interrogation and charges, until after his trial and execution.

In addition, there were the claims from Preucil's father that his son was being held as a British agent and that in 1945, he had been in contact with a British radio station called 'Coctail'. (Where did this information come from? It almost certainly came from the lips of Preucil when his father visited him in Pankrác Prison, but was it true and did the Czech authorities know this?)

The British had been closely aligned to the Czechoslovakian government in exile, while thousands of men had fought in the Free Czech forces based in Britain. The SOE had trained and sent numerous Czech agents to the country, and they had killed Reinhard Heydrich in 1942. The British had also sought, via the Swiss Red Cross, to protect captured Czech RAFVR men in 1941 and again in 1944. So why did they not keep the British updated about Preucil?

There are possibly three separate reasons:

1. The Czech authorities really did think he was a British agent. If they were not aware of his presence and actions, they may have believed he was working against his own countrymen – especially if he was betraying others and sending them to their deaths (as the evidence proved).
2. In the May 1945 Uprising, (the same uprising in which the Chetnik Terezín prison warden was killed), the Soviet army was sweeping in from the east across Czechoslovakia. The American Third Army under General Patton entered the country from the west, but

the Nazis still controlled Prague. In less than a week, the bloodletting in the capital and its surrounding areas amounted to the deaths of about 3,000 Czechs and Germans. Eisenhower did not want to risk casualties by pushing the US Army into Prague and after a few days, the uprising ended with the Soviet army entering the city. The Czech's saw the perceived lack of support from the western powers, alongside the pre-war Munich Agreement, as an indication the Western Allies did not care about Czechoslovakia. This feeling continued until 1948, when the communists took control of the nation. This, therefore, could have been the reason for a lack of communication with Britain over the Preucil affair.
3. The third reason is that the Czechoslovakian government and their air force were too ashamed and embarrassed by Preucil's actions to inform the British.

In all likelihood, the Czechoslovakian government and their prosecuting authorities possibly had an element of anti-Western feeling in their deliberations, especially after 1945. It is worth remembering that as early as 20 May 1945, in his first interview, Preucil had claimed not only to be an English agent, but also that the English were against the Russians who now effectively controlled Czechoslovakia. (A year after Preucil's execution, Czech Communists aligned with the Soviet Union did indeed take control of the country.)

There is no doubt that Preucil worked for the Gestapo in Poland and probably in France. On these charges alone, Preucil probably deserved his final fate.

While this appears to be an open and shut case, and Preucil was tried and executed in Prague in 1947, there are a number of unresolved questions:

1. Did Preucil continue to work for the Gestapo in Britain?
2. Was he identified and 'turned' by the British SIS?
3. Was his unidentified wife's brother-in-law his SIS contact?
4. Was he trained in intelligence work and counter-interrogation techniques?
5. Was he just repeating what he heard from the likes of Čurda and Gerik?
6. Was Karel Richter sent to train and equip Preucil?
7. Was the stolen Hurricane a cover for an SIS operation?
8. Was he part of an SIS anti-SOE operation?
9. Did the Czech's fail to communicate with the British, because they were moving towards the Soviets and believed Preucil to be a British agent?
10. Why is there no known 'open' SIS file on Preucil or even his flight to Belgium available for viewing?

We may never answer any of the ten questions, but the fact remains that the full story of Augustin Preucil will probably never be known and will remain a mystery forever.

Appendix One

Sergeant Augustin Preucil's flights with 'A' Flight, 43 Squadron RAF

Date	Hours	Type of Flight	Accompanied by
10 October 1940	17.25-18.00	Formation flying	FTL Atkinson & SGT Rudolf Ptacek
11 October 1940	11.25-12.20	Formation flying	FTL Frank Carey & SGT Oldrich Fiafa
	15.25-15.50	Aerobatics	SGT Oldrich Fiafa
12 October 1940	10.25-11.00	Formation flying & attacks	FTL Frank Carey
	11.35-12.25	Formation flying & attacks	FTL Frank Carey & SGT Oldrich Fiafa
13 October 1940	15.00-15.50	Formation flying	PO Langdon & SGT Oldrich Fiafa Preucil returned 20 minutes late?
16 October 1940	14.30-15.25	Formation flying & attacks	FTL Frank Carey & 4 others
18 October 1940	14.00-14.45	Formation flying	FTL Kilmartin & 2 others
19 October 1940	11.20-12.20	Formation flying	PO Langdon & SGT Fiafa
24 October 1940	10.25-11.25	Formation flying & attacks	FTL Frank Carey & SGT Oldrich Fiafa
24 October 1940	14.10-15.10	Formation flying	FTL Kilmartin & SGT Oldrich Fiafa
24 October 1940	16.15-16.35	Air climb	SGT Oldrich Fiafa

Date	Hours	Type of Flight	Accompanied by
25 October 1940	14.30–15.25	Formation flying	FTL Atkinson SGT Oldrich Fiafa & 3 others
28 October 1940	10.40–11.20	Aerobatics	Alone
	12.10–11.30	Formation flying	FTL Atkinson & SGT Oldrich Fiafa
31 October 1940	10.25–11.30	Aerobatics & attacks	FTL Frank Carey & SGT Fiafa
31 October 1940	12.10–12.45	Air combat & aerobatics	SGT Oldrich Fiafa
1 November 1940	10.10–11.05	Formation quarter attack	FTL Frank Carey & SGT Oldrich Fiafa
1 November 1940	15.00–15.25	Target attacks	FTL Frank Carey, SGT Oldrich Fiafa & one other
2 November 1940	09.10–10.30	High Altitude flying	FTL Atkinson & SGT Oldrich Fiafa
2 November 1940	11.15–11.55	Air combat	SGT Oldrich Fiafa
3 November 1940	10.30–11.05	Aerobatics	Alone
	14.00–14.50	Altitude flying	Alone
4 November 1940	13.25–14.00	Air combat	SGT Joseph Pipa
8 November 1940	15.50–16.20	Aerobatics	Alone
10 November 1940	13.45–15.00	Formation flying	SGT Joesph Pipa
	15.35–16.25	Air combat	SGT Oldrich Fiafa
11 November 1940	09.20–10.00	Aerobatics	Alone
	11.10–12.25	Local flight	Alone
12 November 1940	11.45–12.40	Climb to 30,000ft	Alone

Appendix Two

Gestapo Officials linked to this story

Heinz Diabo (b. 10 October 1910): Chief Criminal section of Prague Gestapo. Deputy to Heinz Pannwitz in section IIG; from November 1943 official in section IV 2.

Oskar Fleischer (b. 7 December 1892): before the war Chief of Gestapo in Annaberg and also Abwher official in Dresden. One of the most brutal in Prague and ran Preucil as an agent. Fled post-war and he was allegedly found living in West Germany in the 1960s.

Adolf Fuchs (b. 8 February 1909): former Chief of Gestapo in Cologne, then official at section II B in Prague Gestapo; from November 1941 Chief of the Gestapo in Budweis (Eeske Budijovice); from Dec. 1943 Chief of section II BM in Prague.

Josef Chalupský (b. 27 January 1901): former police officer then Gestapo interpreter given German citizenship, active against Heydrich assassins and became a post-war StB agent in Czechoslovakia.

Klaus Petereit (date of birth unknown): Gestapo Secretary who escorted Preucil back to Prague in 1941.

Willi/Wilhelm Leimer (b. 25 July 1912): former engineer he became a Russian NKVD agent inside the Gestapo. Led

Gestapo anti-communist section and in 1942–45 the Gestapo anti-parachutist unit responsible for the deaths of hundreds of Czech resistance fighters. Fled to Russia and joined KGB post war; Stalin awarding him the Order of Lenin. However, others claim he was arrested in May 1945 and executed in Prague on 12 October 1945.

Heinz Pannwitz (b. 8 July 1901): from August 1939 Chief of section II G in Prague Gestapo. When Heydrich was assassinated, both Pannwitz and Fleischer had the 'best' arrest numbers. From September 1942 he was in Unit ZbV of Special Commando 'Brandenberg 800' in the Leningrad. From January 1943 he was in Berlin and then France. Post-war he fled to Russia and joined the NKVD, before returning to West Germany where he died in 1975.

Wilhelm Schultze (b. 18 September 1909): veterinarian by trade; from 1941 Chief of the 3rd Section of Prague Gestapo; built intelligence team but unaccounted for in 1945. Believed by some to work for British secret service.

Josef Vesely (date of birth unknown): Gestapo agent in the anti-parachutist section. Sentenced post-war to eight years imprisonment. Died in 1986.

Jaroslav Nachtmann (b. 1 November 1915): former dentist, Czech police and boxer. Received German citizenship and joined Gestapo section II BM in Prague with Adolf Fuchs and Bedřich Bauer. Bodyguard for Karl Frank before joining the anti-parachutist section in November 1942. He went to Russia where he was sentenced to fifteen years' hard labour. Later joined KGB but rearrested and handed over to Czech StB.

Steinbarth/Steinwardt (date of birth unknown): criminal secretary Benešov Gestapo.

Vilibalda Burgeho/Bunge (date of birth unknown): criminal secretary Prague Gestapo.

Jiri Pitter (date of birth unknown): Prague Gestapo official 1941-45.

Oswald Marx (b. 14 February 1911): Gestapo interpreter in Prague and Section II BM; executed in February 1947.

Hugo Heller (date of birth unknown): Gestapo office assistant and interpreter in Prague.

Karel Herschelmann (date of birth unknown): Gestapo Kommissar in Prague with Fleischer, section III, IV 1b 2a.

Bedřich Bauer (date of birth unknown): Chief Criminal Assistant. Started in Tabor from 17 March 1939 to section II BM in Prague.

Jan Metzner (date of birth unknown): Criminal Assistant section III and IV Prague.

Julius Reidel Muller (b. 26 May 1907): Inspektor Gestapo Prague, then Criminal secretary May 1944 to May 1945 in Benešov. Executed 6 December 1946.

Appendix Three

Czechoslovak/SOE (Arisaig) backed parachutist operations 1941–42

Codename: Benjamin
Otmar Riedl
Dropped with codes and radio parts on 16/17 April 1941. He was not identified as a parachutist and only charged with making an illegal border crossing. He managed to remain undercover and survived the war.

Codename: Percentage
Corporal František Pavelka +
Dropped with a radio and secret-ciphers for 'home army' on 4 October 1941. Arrested on 25 October in Prague and interrogated by the Gestapo at their Petschek Palace headquarters. He was sent to Berlin and guillotined on 11 January 1943. It is possible he had contact with Augustin Preucil, but no evidence can be found to corroborate this. He was promoted while detained and commissioned.

Codename: Anthropoid
Sergeant Josef Gabcik +
Sergeant Jan Kubis +
Directed to kill Reinhardt Heydrich, dropping on 28/29 December 1941. After carrying out the successful attack, they

---
+ killed in action or executed

sought refuge in the church in Resslova Street where they died on 18 June 1942. The deceased men had their heads severed and displayed to their families.

Codename: Silver 'A'
Lieutenant Alfred Bartos +
Sergeant Josef Valcik +
Corporal Jiri Potucek +
Dropped on 28/29 December 1941 with orders to establish intelligence networks and prepare for further arrivals. Josef Valcik assisted the Anthropoid operation and died at the church. Lieutenant Bartos was cornered at a safe house on 21 June 1942. He attempted to commit suicide, but only mortally wounded himself, dying the following day. Corporal Jiri Potucek went on the run and was shot dead by Czech police while hiding in bushes on 2 August 1942.

Codename: Silver 'B'
Sergeant Vladimir Skacha
Sergeant Jan Zemek
Dropped on 28/29 December 1941 to deliver a radio transmitter to a resistance group and to arrange further weapons drops. They went into hiding when they lost their equipment. Skacha was located by the Gestapo in December 1944 but managed to escape during a shoot-out. However, he was detained on 3 January 1945 and sent to the Flossenburg concentration camp. He survived and was liberated by the US Army. Jan Zemek avoided capture and worked with partisans.

Codename: Zinc
Lieutenant Oldrich Pechal +
Sergeant Arnost Miks +
Corporal Viliam Gerik (Executed post-war)
Dropped with orders to link up with Silver 'B' they became separated and Lieutenant Pechal became involved in a fire-fight with German Customs officers and was detained as a suspected black-market smuggler. He escaped from custody, killing one German officer and went on the run. He was eventually detained after a collaborator betrayed him and two priests who were sheltering him. He was tortured before being sent to Mauthausen concentration camp where he was hanged on 22 September 1942.

Arnost Miks, with the help of his resident brother, obtained new identification documents and went to Prague where he tried to locate the Bivouac (see later) group equipment. However, the authorities were waiting and he shot two officers and was wounded himself. Rather than be detained, he committed suicide.

Viliam Gerik gave himself up at a Czech police station, but they immediately handed him over to the Gestapo. He became a Gestapo agent and assisted them greatly, associating with Karel Čurda and Augustin Preucil. He gave evidence in the case of Preucil, and was executed after the war by hanging.

Codename: Out-Distance
Lieutenant Adolf Opalka +
Sergeant Karel Čurda (Executed post-war)
Corporal Ivan Kolarik +
Dropped on 27/28 March 1942 with orders to assist the RAF bombing of the Skoda works in Pilzen, Corporal Kolarik was detained by the Gestapo in Brno and committed suicide.

Lieutenant Opalka joined the Anthropoid team and was killed in the church on 18 June 1942, while Čurda, who had sought shelter with his family, feared Gestapo/SS reprisals against his community and went to the Gestapo to give information. Although he did not know of the church hiding place, he knew safe houses, which were raided by the Gestapo. Those arrested were tortured and gave the location of the church and the seven parachutists.

Codename: Bivouac
Sergeant František Pospisil +
Sergeant Jindrich Coupek +
Corporal Libor Zapletal +
Dropped on the night of 27/28 April 1942 to destroy the rail bridge at Precov as well as the power-station at Brno. Coupek and Zapletal hid with Coupek's relatives and were discovered by the Gestapo. Coupek was sent to Mauthausen concentration camp where he was hanged on 22 September 1942 with Lieutenant Pechal of the Zinc group.

Zapetal went on the run with Pospisil but he was arrested on 2 May 1942. After the war it was alleged that he collaborated with the Gestapo, but when Heydrich was assassinated, he tried to flee to Switzerland and was arrested. He was sent to Mauthausen concentration camp and hanged there in September 1943.

When Zapetal was arrested in May 1942, Pospisil was wounded but managed to escape. In February 1943, he met Karel Čurda (by now a Gestapo agent) as well as Jaroslav Nachtmann. He went to Prague and was detained by the Gestapo on

12 February 1943. He was sent to Terezín concentration camp and shot by a firing squad on 28 October 1944.

Codename: Bioscope
Sergeant Bohuslav Kouba +
Sergeant Josef Bublik +
Sergeant Jan Hruby +
Sergeant Kouba was detained on 3 May 1942 and committed suicide by poison in his cell. Bublik and Hruby linked up with the Anthropoid group and were killed in the church on 18 June 1942.

Codename: Steel
Lance Corporal Oldrich Dvorak +
Dropped with a radio on 27/28 April 1942; he was betrayed and shot as he tried to escape.

Codename: Intransitive
Lieutenant Vaclav Kindl +
Sergeant Bohuslav Grabovsky +
Corporal Vojtech Lukastik +
Dropped on 29/30 April 1942 to sabotage an oil instillation at Kolin. They lost their equipment in the drop and immediately went into hiding. Kindl and Grabovsky were detained by the Gestapo and agreed to collaborate, however Gravovsky failed to impress and was sent to Terezín concentration camp where he was executed in October 1944 (possibly with Zapetal of the Bivouac group.) Kindl continued to work with the Gestapo and was accidentally hit by gunfire and killed on 20 May 1944.

Lutastik was tracked down by the Gestapo to Jankovice on 8 January 1943 and after a fire-fight, he shot himself.

Codename: Tin
Sergeant Ludvík Cupal +
Sergeant Jaroslav Svarc +
Dropped on 29/30 April 1942 with orders to assassinate the Minister of Education and Propaganda, Emanuel Moravec. The drop was a failure and both men injured. Svarc joined the Anthropoid group and died in the church on 18 June 1942. Cupal evaded capture but shot himself on 15 January 1943 when surrounded at Velehrad.

In total during this period, twelve parachute drops were made consisting of twenty-eight men. A number collaborated with the Gestapo and either died in the service of their new masters or were executed by Czech authorities post-war.

Appendix Four

Captured Czech aircrew held in Prague 1944:
(Bold – confirmed or possibly in contact with Preucil)

Rank/Name	Unit	Role	Captured	PoW Camp	Prague	PoW Camp
PO Bedřich Dvorak	312 Sqn	Pilot	03/06/42	Sagan Escaped 25/03/44 Recaptured 09/04/44	09/04/44	Barth 30/11/44 Colditz 09/01/45
FTL Ivo Tonder	312 Sqn	Pilot	03/06/42	Sagan Escaped 25/03/44 Recaptured 28/03/44 Richenberg	16/04/44	Barth 30/11/44 Colditz 08/01/45
WO Viliam Bufka	311 Sqn	Pilot	22/06/41	Hospital Barth Sagan	23/07/44	Colditz 10/10/44
WO Josef Zvolensky	311 Sqn	W/Op	20/10/41	Lamsdoff Barth Sagan	23/07/44	Barth 18/08/44
WO Petr Uruba	311 Sqn	Pilot	06/02/41	Barth Sagan	23/07/44	Barth 18/08/44 Colditz 10/09/44
FTL Budil Bohuslav	312 Sqn	Pilot	19/04/44	Sagan	03/08/44	Barth 19/8/44
FTL Vaclav Kilian	311 Sqn	A/Gunner	23/09/40	Berlin Tegel Sagan	13/08/44	Barth 19/08/44

Captured Czech aircrew held in Prague 1944

Rank/Name	Unit	Role	Captured	PoW Camp	Prague	PoW Camp
FTL František Burda	310 Sqn	Pilot	27/02/43	Sagan	13/08/44	Barth 19/08/44 Colditz 10/09/44
PO Emil Busina	311 Sqn	Navigator	06/02/41	Barth Sagan	13/08/44	Barth 19/08/44 Colditz 10/09/44
FTL Jaroslav Zafouk	311 Sqn	Navigator	17/07/41	Escaped late 1941. Recaptured Prague 19/06/42 to Colditz	14/08/44	Colditz Sept. 44
FTL Milan František Zapletal	311 Sqn	Navigator	14/04/42	Hospital Sagan	14/08/44	Barth Sept. 44
FTL Karel Josef Trojacek	311 Sqn	Pilot	23/09/40	Berlin Tegel Sagan	14/08/44	Barth 02/09/44 Colditz 09/01/45
FTL Otakar Cerny	311 Sqn	W/Op	17/07/41	Warburg Sagan	14/08/44	Colditz 26/10/44
Sgt Cenek Chaloupka	312 Sqn	Pilot	06/10/41	Barth Colditz	14/08/44	Colditz 31/10/44
FTL František Cigos	311 Sqn	Pilot	06/02/41	Barth Sagan	14/08/44	Barth 09/09/44 Colditz 22/09/44
FTL Zdeněk Prochazka	311 Sqn	Navigator	23/09/41	Berlin Tegel Sagan	14/08/44	Barth 02/09/44
FTL Erazim Vesely	311 Sqn	Pilot	20/10/41	Barth Sagan	14/08/44	Colditz 15/09/44

Rank/Name	Unit	Role	Captured	PoW Camp	Prague	PoW Camp
SGT Karel Batelka	311 Sqn	A/Gunner	17/01/42	Barth	25/08/44	Colditz 22/09/44
WO František Knap	322 Sqn	A/Gunner	17/07/41	Sagan Barth	25/08/44	Barth Sept. 44
WO Emanuel Novotny	311 Sqn	Pilot	16/10/40	Barth Sagan	25/08/44	Barth Sept. 44 Colditz 10/10/44
WO Vaclav Prochazka	311 Sqn	Pilot	20/10/41	Sagan Barth	25/08/44	Barth Sept. 44 Colditz 22/09/44
WO Alois Siska	311 Sqn	Pilot	28/12/41	Hospital Sagan Barth	25/08/44	Barth Sept. 44 Colditz 22/09/44
WO Josef Susa	311 Sqn	A/Gunner	20/10/41	Sagan Barth	25/08/44	Colditz 27/10/44
FO Vaclav Truhlar	313 Sqn	Pilot	10/04/42	Sagan Barth	25/08/44	Colditz Sept. 44
FTL Josef Bryks	242 Sqn	Pilot	17/06/41	Sagan	01/09/44	Barth 22/09/44 Colditz 07/11/44

Resources used in this book

UK National Archives: Contains public sector information accessed under the Open Government Licence

AIR 28/871 RAF Usworth Operations Record Book

AIR 29/682 55 Operational Training Unit's Operations Record Book

AIR 81/9163 Casualty File – Augustine Preucil missing 19/09/1941 Hurricane W9147, 55 OTU

AIR 27/441/22 & 21 Operations Record Book for 43 Squadron RAF (November 1940)

AIR 27/441/19 & 20 Operations Record Book for 43 Squadron RAF (October 1940)

AIR 27/2088/21 & 22 Operations Record books for 605 Squadron RAF (November 1940)

AIR 27/2088/23 & 24 Operations Record books for 605 Squadron RAF (December 1940)

AIR 28/815 Operations Record Book for Tangmere

AIR 28/871 Operations Record Book for Usworth

AIR 29/978 Operations Record Book for 18 MU

KV2/31, KV2/32 & KV2/33 MI5 files for agent Karel Richter

KV/225 & KV2/26 MI5 files for agent Josef Jakobs

Regional Archives in Prague, Czech Republic:
Investigation and trial transcripts for Augustin Preucil

Czech Prison records:
Post-arrest photographic image

RAF Museum Hendon:
Form AM 1180 – Accident Card for Hurricane W9147
Form AM 1180 – Accident card for Hurricane V7608

RAF Personnel records branch:
Personal file for Sergeant Augustin Preucil RAF No. 787344

RAF Air Historical Branch: (Dr Alastair Noble)

UK National Registry (National Archives):
Marriage Certificate for Preucil & Murial Graham Kirby (British records)
Death certificate of Murial Graham Kirby (née Preucil) (British records)

Media:
The Evening News, Tuesday, 15 April 1947
The Times newspaper, Wednesday, 16 April 1947
Flypast magazine, December 2001 and January 2002
Aeroplane magazine, June 2003

Miscellaneous:
www.nelsam.org.uk/NEAR/Research.htm – North East Aircraft Museum / research
www.rafaci.cz – Czechoslovak pilots in the RAF in WW2 website. (Josef 'Joe' Vochyán)

www.fcafa.com- Free Czechoslovak Air Force Association
www.belgians-remember-them.eu- Belgian Resistance website and 'Clarence' group

Bibliography:

Hodder, Petra, *In the Heavens and in Hell* (2018) Mustang publishing (Czech Republic)

Pearson, Simon, *The Great Escaper* (2013) Hodder & Stoughton Ltd

Index

Adamek (Lieutenant), 126
Airfields (Czech):
   Hradec Kralove, 3, 22
   Prostejov, 2, 22, 34, 88, 154, 163
Ambrus, Jan (Squadron Leader/Major), 162, 173
Apson (Gestapo informant), 84

Bella, Jaroslav (Captain), 152
Benes, Eduard (President), 35, 43, 101
Benešov (town), 78–83, 106–14, 128, 170, 223
Brantal, Max, 27–8, 40–1, 46, 53–61, 100–102, 117, 120–1, 129, 134, 136, 139, 143
Brejcha, Vaclav (Sergeant), 34
Brejcha (Terezín prisoner), 90
Brno (town), 65, 118, 121–2, 226–7
Bruhns, Dr, 204
Bufka, Viliam (Flight Sergeant), 149, 157
Burda, František (Flight Lieutenant/Captain), 51, 145–9, 152–6, 164

Bushell, Roger (Squadron Leader), 158–61

Cadil Bohuslav, 41, 46–7, 58, 78–9, 103–115
Cameron (Group Captain), 191–2
Canaris, Wilhelm, 201
Carey, Frank (Flight Lieutenant), 7
Charlier, Leon, 17
Cisovice (town), 28
Clarence (Resistance), 16, 172
Coctail (Radio network), 178, 181, 216
Čurda, Karel (Sergeant/SOE), 19, 26–30, 37–43, 48, 51, 55–6, 61–8, 74, 91, 97, 115–8, 127–9, 145, 161, 174, 194, 218, 226–7

David, Jan, 82
Davle (Town), 19–20
Dejvice (Town), 74–5, 138
Dostalova, Maria, 108–109
Drabek, Jaroslav (Prosecutor), 192

Duda, Josef (Flight Lieutenant/Captain), 31, 35, 163–4
Durand, Armand, 17

Ebr, Karel, 100
Engler, Vaclav (General), 23, 44, 125–7

Fiafa, Oldrich (Sergeant), 7–8
Fortikova, Ella, 28, 43, 45, 58, 132, 135–6, 140–4
Fuller, Pepik (Sergeant), 23

Gerik, Viliam (Corporal/SOE), 19, 26–30, 36–43, 48–51, 55–6, 61–9, 74–6, 91, 115–29, 145, 159–60, 174, 194, 215, 218, 226
Gestapo officers & officials:
  Bauer, Bedřich, 29, 73, 76, 84, 159, 160, 222
  Bodenschatz, Karl (General), 171, 200
  Burgeho, Vilibalda, 77–8
  Chalupský, Josef (Interpreter), 26, 46, 49, 56, 70–6, 93, 117–20, 196, 199–201
  Darido, 45
  David, Bohuslav, 29, 81–3
  Diabo, Heinz, 29, 65–6
  Eska, Josef, 80–1, 91–3
  Fleischer, Oskar, 4, 29, 65, 68, 70–6, 84, 159–60, 201
  Frank, Karl, 18, 222
  Fuchs, Adolf, 29, 222
  Heller, Hugo, 77–80, 109
  Herschelmann, Karel, 71–6
  Jockel, Heinrich (Terezín Commandant), 91
  Kain, 130
  Leimer, Wilhelm, 29, 49, 70, 75–6
  Marx, Oswald, 79–80
  Metzner, Jan, 29
  Muller, Julius, 29, 223
  Nachtmann, Jaroslav, 39, 70, 222, 227
  Pitter, Jiri, 29, 76, 84
  Schaub, Julius, 171, 200
Glowacki, Antoni (Sergeant), 10
Göring, Hermann, 3, 171, 200
Grabovsky, Bohuslav (Sergeant/SOE), 29, 42, 65–7, 115, 145, 228

Hajek, Miroslav, 41, 45, 57–9, 100–107
Hanus, Josef (Brigadier General), 186–7
Hanzlicek, Otto (Sergeant), 34
Haranice (Town), 24
Hess, Alexander (Squadron Leader/Major), 32, 126, 152
Heydrich, Reinhard, 19, 28, 37–8, 40, 49, 55, 62, 65, 70, 88, 90, 118, 123, 127, 161, 201–202, 216

Himmler, Heinrich, 200
Hinkley-Cooke, William E. (SIS), 208
Hlaváček, Karel, 91, 97–9
Hofmeister, Dr., 168–70
Holic (Terezín barber), 81, 92–3, 98
Honza, Svobada, 23
Hradistek, 1
Hurt, Josef (Professor), 78–9, 106–109, 113, 115
Husova Street, Ziskov, 28
Hvoznice (Town), 107, 137

Ingra (General), 81, 92

Jakobs, Josef, 209–10
Janousek, G. (General), 17, 172–3
Jerhot, Karel (Čurda's alias), 27, 38, 55, 66
Jindra (Czech resistance group), 38

Kembal, (Lieutenant), 35
Kindl, Vaclav (Lieutenant/SOE), 29, 42, 65–7, 115, 145, 194, 228
Kirby, George, 11
Kirby, Muriel G., 11–12, 18, 32, 150, 172–95
Koci, František (Defending lawyer), 21, 170

Kolomaznik, Alois, 89–90
Kopecke, 44, 127
Kordula, (Colonel), 150
Kotnik, Josef, 128–9
Krajina, Vladimir (Doctor & Terezín prisoner), 43, 81, 90–3, 97–9
Kratochvila (General), 44, 126
Kunka, (Sergeant), 146

Langdon, Charles (Pilot Officer), 8
Libensky, Stanislav, 102
Liberec (Town), 92, 158
Libno (Town), 44, 83
Livingston, A.W. (Air Ministry), 189–90
Long (Squadron leader Air Intelligence), 18
Luke, Emil (Terezín prisoner), 43, 81, 91–7

Machacek (Lieutenant), 47
Malik, Ivan, 40, 56
Mechenice (Town), 19–20, 41, 47, 58, 78, 88, 103, 105–109, 112–13, 127, 135, 142–4
Mellan, Jaroslav (Defending lawyer), 21, 170
Mikovsky, 23, 48, 71
Miller (Captain), 41
Modrak, Vaclav (Sergeant), 27, 40, 49, 55–6, 116–17, 121–4

Na Ruska inn, Libno, 83
Němec, Ludovick (Trebsin Police Stn. Commander), 85–8, 125, 160
Nejedly, Karel (Terezín warden), 92–3, 98
Nouville, Francie Plukovnik, 32

Opalka, Adolf (Lieutenant/ SOE), 39, 226–7
Osusky, Stefan, 35–6

Petrina, 44, 82–4
Pierrepoint, Albert, 208
Piestan, 2, 22
Pinca, 92, 97
Pipa, Josef (Sergeant), 7
Pospisil, František (Sergeant/ SOE), 29, 39, 62, 227
Povolny, Augustin, 44, 127
Prague:
  Breddovska Street, 83
  Bulovka hospital, 44, 114, 168–70
  Chechova Street, 129
  Rolny store, 3, 104, 133, 138
  Koruna Arcade, 39
  Krizovnicke Street, 57
  Metro/Vagon restaurant, 101, 136, 139
  Prisak store, 138
  Resslove Street (St Cyril's church), 38, 55, 69, 118, 225
  Rytirska Street, 128–6, 135
  Spalena Street, 60
  Trznica restaurant, 128
  Vela Market Place, 58
  Veletrzny Palace, 44, 125
  Vinohradske, 149
  Vodickova Street, 3, 138
Preizler, Jan, 134–7
Preucil, Marie, 1, 20, 44, 142–4, 170, 181
Prkal (Sergeant), xi
Provaznik (Captain), 32
Ptacek, Rudolf (Sergeant), 7

RAF airfields & Units;
  Aldergrove No. 23 MU, 8–9, 15
  Cosford, 6, 150, 152, 155, 162–5, 197
  Dumfries No. 18 MU, 9, 15
  Hullavington No. 10 MU, 9, 11, 15
  Kemble No 4 Ferry Pilots, 9, 15, 31, 211
  Little Rissington No. 8 MU, 31
  Sutton Bridge 6 OTU, 6–10, 15, 155, 165, 182, 197–200
  Usworth, 7–12, 15, 21, 25, 29, 34, 147, 155–6, 165, 182, 197–200
  310 Squadron, 32, 151, 155, 161, 186, 198, 231

311 Squadron, 145, 148, 157, 230–2
312 Squadron, 31, 34, 158, 162–5, 198, 230–1
43 Squadron, 7–11, 13–15, 32–4, 155, 165, 219
55 OTU, 10–15, 147
605 Squadron, 8, 198–9
Razga, V. (Gen. Consul UK), 184
Reed, Ronald Thomas (SIS), 207–9
Rehak, Vaclav, 2, 20–2, 149
Rejthar, Stanislav (Squadron Leader/Major), 147–50
Reporyje, 102
Richter, Karel, 202–18
Robertson, Thomas Argyll (SIS), 207
Ropeznik (Captain), 47
Royce, Elliott (Flight Lieutenant), xi

Saifer, Olda, 28
Schmidt, Wulf, 202, 206, 210
Seignet, 178
Senflok (place), 23, 41, 56, 95
Shreeve, I.G. (RAF Casualty Bureau), 174
Sichovsky, Zdeněk (Sergeant), 147–8, 153

Šifner, Karel (Squadron Leader/Major), 31, 34–6, 153, 173
Sifrou, Josef (Preucil's alias), 107
Skvor, Ladislav, 47, 80, 107, 112–15
Smetana, Bedřich, 24, 28, 32, 48, 71
Smetana, František, 71
SOE Operations:
 Intransive, 42, 228
 Out Distance, 37, 226
 Zinc, 36, 226–7
Stamp, Frank (Sergeant RCAF), 12–13
Standera, Miroslav (Sergeant), 148, 164–5
Stehlik, Josef (Sergeant), 106, 148, 164
Strzinek, 28
Svaska, Laislava, 139

Taskovi (Colonel), 128
Tomanova, Jarmila, 116, 121
Tomanova, Karel, 56, 121, 123
Tomanova, Milena, 27, 40–9, 55–6, 69, 74–6, 116, 132, 142, 194, 215
Tonder, Ivo (Flight Lieutenant/Captain), 149, 157–9

Index 241

Trebsin (Village), 1, 20, 26, 36, 43, 51–4, 58, 85–8, 96, 112, 127, 142, 147, 160, 177, 191–4
Tuma, Josef (Terezín prisoner), 43, 91–6
Tumove, Jirina, 137

Ukaur, Oldrich, 129
Uruby, Petr (Captain), 157

Vancurova, Jaroslava, 129
Vaneta, Vaclav (Police inspector), 86
Vanisova, Jarina, 45, 107, 132–42

Vasmut, 178
Vesel Alois, 137
Vitejcek, Josef, 109–15
Vnouck, František, 86
Vohryzek, František, (Dr Justice), 176

Warner, S.J. (Red Cross), 182
Wyatt, G.M. (Group Captain Prague Attache), 186–8

Zeithammel family, 159–60
Zbraslav (Place), 45, 78, 134
Zima, Rudolf (Flight Lieutenant/Captain), 149–52